A Southwest Landmark

Number Two

13
DAYS TO GLORY

DAYS TO GLORY

THE SIEGE OF THE ALAMO

by Lon Tinkle

Texas A&M University Press, *College Station*

Originally published in 1958 by McGraw-Hill Book Company, Inc.,
New York, Toronto, and London.

Tinkle, Lon.
  13 days to glory.

  (A Southwest landmark; no.2)
  Reprint. Originally published: New York: McGraw-
Hill 1958.
  Bibliography: p.
  1. Alamo (San Antonio, Tex.)—Siege, 1836. 2. Texas
—History—Revolution, 1835–1836. I. Title. II. Title:
Thirteen days to glory. III. Series.
F390.T5   1985   976.4'03   85-40043
ISBN 0-89096-238-3; 0-89096-707-5 (pbk.)

Manufactured in the United States of America
Seventh printing, 1999

For MARIA, and our three sons:
JON, ALAN, and ANTHONY

ACKNOWLEDGMENTS

Like many another writer on the Southwest, I have profited from the generosity of three noted historians: J. Frank Dobie, Paul Horgan, and Walter Prescott Webb. To them is due in large part whatever credit this book may claim.

I am indebted as well to Herbert Gambrell, director of the Texas Hall of State, and his wife Virginia, whose comments, like those of Karle Wilson Baker, were invaluable. To Carlos Castañeda of the University of Texas, for helping me with Mexican sources, and to Miss Ruby Mixon of Fort Worth, for guiding me in Travis material, I owe special debts of gratitude.

I am also grateful to those descendants of Alamo families—Mrs. J. Leonard Smith of Dallas, and Mrs. William Campbell and Mrs. Frank C. Gillespie of San Antonio —who furnished me with valuable material. Miss Nina Hill, Mrs. Eugene McDermott, Mrs. Starkey Duncan, Miss Maria De Haro, William H. Kittrell, and R. G. Hartman were also helpful.

To librarians I share the common debt of all researchers. Miss Marg-riette Montgomery of the Alamo Library, Mrs. R. G. Halter of the Alamo Museum, Misses Llerena Friend and Winnie Allen of the Eugene C. Barker Center at Austin, Mrs. Frances Horton of the Texas State Library, and Mrs. B. A. Brandt of the Texas State Archives were of enormous aid to me. In Dallas, Max Trent, Lois Bailey, James Meeks, and Mrs. Margaret Pratt made my path easier; as did Jess McNeel, Arthur Coleman, Albert Curtis, and the staff of the San Antonio Public Library. I am especially indebted to Mrs. Marie Petersen and Mrs. Ollie Crenshaw, custodians of the Texas collection of the *Dallas Morning News*, and to Donald Gallup, curator of the Yale American collection. My very great debt to my editors, Ed Kuhn and Robert Hutchinson, must also be mentioned.

I should like in particular to single out my late friend, E. DeGolyer of Dallas, for letting me use his private library and teaching me more than he realized. The late George Sessions Perry verified two stories for me. Of my colleagues at the *Dallas Morning News*, Sam Acheson and Paul Crume were steady supports, as were Allen Maxwell and Miss Anne Wright. At Southern Methodist University, finally, I incurred obligations too numerous to mention.

I owe them all more than I can say.

Lon Tinkle

CONTENTS

LIST OF ILLUSTRATIONS

following page 128

At ten o'clock on the morning of February 23, 1836, a sentry named Daniel William Cloud was standing in the bell tower of San Fernando Church in San Antonio looking along the western horizon for movement. He was twenty-one years old, he had been standing there for three hours under orders from James Bowie and William Barret Travis, and every time he faced the white glare of the Texas landscape, it looked exactly the same—bare, thorny, and cold. He wondered why he had ever left Kentucky for this empty land.

By all rights he should have been in Missouri. He had started out for there only a few months ago, and his family thought he was there now, beginning his fortune as a young lawyer in young Saint Louis. But somehow his plans had changed. Doors of opportunity kept opening before him. He smiled, wondering whether his mother had received his letter yet. He had sent her a message Christmas Day, two months before, telling her his reasons—how there was not as much law practice in Saint Louis, with its two thousand people, as he had expected; how the farm land in Missouri was not like Kentucky's; how it was in Texas that things were happening, in Texas that a handful of Americans had risen up against tyranny to demand their promised statehood and, denied that by the Mexican government of General Santa Anna, freedom. A hundred youths new in San Antonio like himself shared this contagion, gathered here from all over the States. Now, stamping his feet in the cold of the San Fernando bell tower, he wondered whether it was as good an idea as it seemed at the time. It was something new in his experience not to feel sure.

For one thing, until this morning nothing had happened in Texas since he had been in it. In the six weeks since he had enlisted at Nacogdoches and been sent here, nothing had happened but a parade or two and some crazy dances that went on all night. He yawned, tired at the mere thought of yesterday's rollicking fandango celebrating George Washington's birthday. It would probably be going on yet if it hadn't been for the sudden shower at midnight and that message urgently handed to Jim Bowie, the message that made Bowie and Travis station him in the bell tower. But fatigue might have stopped it anyway. February 22 had been a mighty long stretch, with Davy Crockett's southern-fried oratory starting at noon, with the *tamales* and *mescal* Jim Bowie had got his Mexican friends to offer on food-burdened tables set up in Main Plaza, with the dancing and guitar music and fiddle contest, and the horse races and cock fights on the side.

Daniel William Cloud was scanning the hard brown countryside of San Antonio de Béxar now because the message Jim Bowie received had reported that General Santa Anna himself and several thousand troops had, unbelievably, pitched camp the day before on the Medina River, only a few miles south of the mission-fortress Alamo. He had not been expected, if at all, before the middle of March, three weeks off.

If the report were true, it meant fighting, and Daniel Cloud wholeheartedly approved. Other Texans had seen real fighting in December, when they had routed Santa Anna's elegant and dandified brother-in-law, General Martín Perfecto de Cós, and made him and his defeated troops run like jack rabbits to the other side of the Rio Grande. But there had been no more of that since Cós had slunk away in surrender. With no Mexican troops left in Texas, the men in the Texan army didn't even bother about drill or roll call any more. They just ate and slept and chased *señoritas* and sat around the *cantinas* speculating about the feud between the outfit's two commanders. Bowie and Travis, the perennial topics—and recently Davy Crockett for comedy relief.

Even Santa Anna had become a joke, and no one took seriously any longer the rumors that he was on his way, that he had crossed the Rio Grande driving his disconsolate brother-in-law Cós before him, that the Mexican commander was actually camped on the Medina River right now. That was the hardest one of all to believe, though Jim Bowie had seemed to believe it when he halted the dance last night. Everyone knew that the Mexican President-General would never think of moving north over the semidesert between San Antonio and Saltillo in the middle of winter. Everyone knew he would wait for spring, just as Colonel Travis said.

A sudden movement in Main Plaza below alerted the sentry. Instantly he stood frozen, ready to grab the bell rope. Then he grinned, seeing the familiar tall form of Jim Bowie.

Private Cloud liked Bowie, liked him a lot better than Travis, the other commander, who seemed at the same time sad and superior, aloof and shy, hardly human at all with his stern young face and the eyes that seldom let you know what he was thinking. But Jim Bowie—there was a man! When Jim Bowie was around, you knew who was in command, and as though by natural right. Natural right was the slogan of the pioneering Texans. Nature was what they had most of.

The sun shone bright through the clouds breaking in the north and east now, with the promise of warm sunshine to spice the frosty air, and the sentry resumed his watch over the countryside around San Antonio de Béxar —the flat country dense with mesquite thicket south and west, the rolling hills to the north, the San Antonio River that snaked east through the town. For a moment his eye rested on the Alamo, the mission that rose out of the hardstamped earth a scant half-mile east, its handful of buildings barely catching the morning sun inside the rectangular outer walls. He could just make out the small fluted columns in the front of the chapel, flanking the four niches for statues, the chief one of course for Saint Anthony in whose honor it was named, though rarely called, San Antonio de Valero.

Churches in Texas, the young sentry knew, had a way of getting fused with the military. Here he was in

San Fernando's tower for no purpose of prayer or worship. He remembered to look quickly again southwestward for the enemy. He saw nothing but the familiar emptiness, save for the small town below him, whose population of 4,000 were nearly all Mexican. Then Daniel Cloud stifled another yawn and looked away. He was cold, up so high, and tired from the fandangos of the past two nights. And churches did not particularly interest him.

JIM BOWIE was of all men in San Antonio de Béxar the one most worried. The message he had received last night at the dance was far from the first such warning. For two months there had been rumors, vague murmurs impossible to verify, mostly wrong—but maybe, as Bowie suspected, right. The report, for example, from his loyal young Mexican scouts that the bakeries in the border towns below the Rio Grande were flourishing with overwork—what could the report mean except that Santa Anna was getting ready to move—that even now well-stocked troops might be on the march? But how explain that to his fellow Texans who never really knew or wanted to know Mexicans or what was in their complicated minds?

Jim Bowie, entering the Alamo courtyard now, knew Mexicans: in his marriage and in his work he knew them from long understanding and experience—from the friendly San Antonians who had executed *cachuchas* and *jarabes* last night in honor of *El Señor Jorge* Washington, on down to the ones like Santa Anna, the ones who would always, in any land, be the enemy.

It was not the same with Travis, the well-dressed and

finical Travis who at heart disapproved of Bowie and who was repelled by Bowie's thirst for liquor and his reckless laugh. Travis echoed the provisional Texas government's Governor Henry Smith: he would never trust the Mexicans. His premature attack on the Anáhuac customs house last summer had brought nearer a war which Bowie thought could have been won by diplomacy and brains. Now Travis put his trust—incredibly—in simple grass. The Mexican army would never cross the arid near-desert land before the spring came with its watery grass. The ignorance of the belief brought a frown to Jim Bowie's face. Anybody who belonged to this land knew Santa Anna could feed his horses and mules on dry mesquite grass. Bowie had told them himself—how in the long dry autumn the mesquite grass cures as it stands, how it was the best hay you could find. Horses even liked it better, he persisted, liked it better than the juicy grass of spring. But Travis looked at him as if he were drunk again, a look that pitied and condemned at the same time.

A spasm of coughing bent Jim Bowie double, and for a moment he went blind as the coughs racked him. He had no business being out in the February morning air this way, not with the cough he had. His job was inside with Green Jameson, helping to get this old ruin of a mission ready in case they had to defend it. He stopped in an archway for a last warming in the sun. His eye fell on fig trees and oleanders growing around the chapel walls.

It was Travis's mistake, he thought, as he pushed open the heavy door to the headquarters room. Let Travis see what he could do with it.

Travis, who was still in his twenties, while the forty-year-old Bowie held title to almost a million acres of Texas land. . . .

COLONEL WILLIAM BARRET TRAVIS, co-commander of the forces at Béxar, always stopped to talk to the Rodriguez family if he saw them on his way through town to the Alamo. Travis liked children, and the Rodriguez house, the last one before the bridge, offered a convenient place to stop and relax. Like most of his men, he had preferred since his return to Béxar three weeks before to keep quarters in town rather than live in the moldering old mission fortress they had held since taking it from General Cós the previous December. It was more peaceful outside, just as it was more peaceful stopping here to pat the *muchachos* on the head and listen to what their father had to say than going into the Alamo to face Jim Bowie. Ambrosio Rodriguez might be gloomy and full of warnings, but he was always polite.

The twenty-seven-year-old South Carolinian needed politeness. He had not been a commander, he told himself, with a commander's responsibilities, much of his life. Today, though, he did not see any of the Rodriguez children at play. Just as well, perhaps, for it would not be pleasant, after last night's party and the fantastic message for Bowie, to hear the Mexican go on and on about his favorite subject: how the Texans should leave the Alamo and fall back on the American settlements—or Anglo-American, as they were called here, to distinguish their occupants from other Americans to the south who had an equal right to the name. For a week now Ambrosio had been giving him detailed information about Santa Anna's movements—so far all of it correct—and at great risk to himself. He was one of twenty-five San Antonians risking their lot with Jim Bowie, serving in a company organized by Juan Seguin. He would, after all, be considered a traitor in the eyes of the Mexican government. He had a right to be heard.

But his argument was childish. The town of Béxar, Ambrosio never tired of saying, could support neither man nor beast. Cós himself had been starved out, unable to feed his horses after the Texans had burned the prairies during their siege. And the town itself—what could it possibly provide the troops after the last contingent of two hundred Texans had gone off to Matamoros, draining the town of food and the Alamo of powder, men, and medicines?

Travis always smiled at that. Ambrosio was forever insisting how foolish this venture had been, this attempt to carry the war into Mexico. And Travis could see the hidden complaint: *you are ruining our land.*

As patiently as possible Travis would attempt to answer. The Texas army, after all, had no money, no other way to stay alive except to live off the neighboring land. As for the danger, it was not, he would explain, as if the 150 men in the Alamo had been abandoned here. Colonel Fannin would be here any minute, with 400 or more men from Goliad. The messenger had gone days ago. They might even arrive that morning. And what of the reinforcements from the other towns? They could come at a moment's notice. Rodriguez worried too much. Did he really believe Santa Anna, a general coached by highly trained veterans of the Napoleonic wars, was going to risk famine and exposure by moving his army in the wintertime? An army could beat many things, but none could beat pneumonia.

And what about food? The three hundred miles between San Antonio and Santa Anna's position south of the Rio Grande at Saltillo offered little forage for men or mounts, now that Texas scouts had set fire to much of it. Would an army that had suffered four successive defeats at Texan hands the autumn before start north in February? Three weeks from now maybe, around March 15. But not now. Thus Travis had written Gov. Smith on February 13.

No, Travis thought, passing his hand over his eyes, it was as well not to repeat that argument again. . . . Still, he missed seeing the Rodriguez children, and as he started over the split-tree-trunk bridge at the end of Main Street and looked back at the house, he realized that all the windows at the side were boarded over and all the possessions removed from the yard. It gave him a strange feeling, looking at the empty house that had always echoed with laughter. He knew other Mexicans had been leaving, leaving for a week now. But he had not expected it of Ambrosio Rodriguez.

As he hesitated and looked up at San Fernando Church where he had posted a sentry, he wondered exactly what Ambrosio's departure might mean.

THERE HAD BEEN in Texas since 1800 a long parade of Anglo-Americans: first, adventurers, horse dealers, Lafitte's pirates, idealists, thieves; and then, after Stephen F. Austin started colonization, frontiersmen, doctors, lawyers, engineers, merchants—men who had come independently for whatever gain or fate awaited them. The settlers that lived now, however, in the region between the Brazos and Colorado rivers had been there only fifteen years. Unlike the early nomads they had come to build up the land. And unlike the others they had been invited by Mexico.

In 1821 *empresario* Stephen F. Austin, carrying a

Spanish grant later confirmed by Mexico's new independent government, had led the settlers into the new country. It was their purpose to found a colony in the wilderness, and they had succeeded admirably. In fifteen years they had done what the Spaniards and Mexicans before them had never been able to do—subdue the Karankawas and Lipan Apaches. In fifteen years they had managed to place 30,000 Anglo-Americans where the Mexicans had been able to place only 4,000, most of these in the single city of Béxar, now known increasingly as San Antonio de Béxar, or simply San Antonio. Towns had sprung up—towns with names like Columbia, Brazoria, Washington-on-the-Brazos —and the land had flourished as never before.

But whose land? Men from many countries had been there—the *conquistadores* of Coronado, moving majestically north toward the kingdom of Quivira; the survivors of the ill-fated expedition of De Soto; La Salle with his melancholy little settlement on the Gulf Coast. The land belonged, finally, to no one—unless to the Indians and nature itself. Spain had claimed it, then France, then dubiously the United States from the Louisiana Purchase, now Mexico, itself only recently free of Spanish rule. Someday perhaps, the settlers told themselves, it would belong to the people who lived there. (They had entered a republic; and were in revolt now against its usurper-dictator.)

But not until the land to the south had been taken care of. Even to the early adventurers, the Mexicans had brought continual trouble. In 1813 they had savagely put down a republican rebellion in the name of Spain. Now, having won their independence in 1821, they were attempting to crush another one in their own name.

There had always been trouble, of course, but before it was short-lived—rebellions put down before they had a chance to grow: the defeat of hotheaded Texan Haden Edwards and his Republic of Fredonia in 1826, for example, which ended almost before it began. But the present grievances had been building steadily, and since 1830 there had been more friction than friendship between the two peoples. A Mexican attempt to shut off American immigration in that year—a death blow to the hopes of the colonists—had been followed by taxes, from which the Texans had generally been exempt. Trade had become impossible, and —especially disheartening to the Americans—Mexican troops began appearing in abundance, garrisoned in Texas towns as the republic to the south made clear its determination to tighten control over the new land. Separate statehood was the only Texan hope, and that was resolutely denied.

Compromise, the friendly Mexicans in San Antonio said. Why can you Texans not live and let live and everyone go his own way, *contento?* But the Texans had compromised enough. No one could compromise after Stephen F. Austin returned from Mexico in September of 1835, his appeal for statehood a worthless scrap of paper in his pocket and the memory of eighteen months of Mexican prison fresh in his mind. Reason could never reach General Antonio Lopez de Santa Anna, the Mexican dictator. The only weapon now was power. More and more of the peace-loving Texans had swung over to Governor Henry Smith and Travis and the War Party. And more and more it became clear that only one course was possible.

They could do it, the men in the Alamo felt, if they had one thing—if they had unity. Without this they were nothing, and a nation of 30,000 people was nothing. To be sure, the forces of General Cós had been defeated last winter. But now the enemy would be prepared. To resist the army of Santa Anna—the 6,000 men perhaps ready to move north at a moment's notice—for that you must be undivided.

Yet already the shadows were lengthening. Only two months before, the Texas government had become two governments, split squarely down the middle by the question of whether to carry the war to Mexico and—if so—who should lead the invasion. Governor Smith wanted to stay out of Mexico and declare absolute independence; the Council wanted to ally with Mexican liberals in the northern Mexican states and preserve—against Santa Anna's usurpation—the 1824 Republic of Mexico. The result was two rival provisional governments, and a splintered army, to meet 6,000 troops.

It was a good thing, the men at the Alamo agreed, that in Washington-on-the-Brazos, as scheduled by the provisional government before its split, the Constitutional Convention was about to convene....

HIGH IN THE BELL TOWER of San Fernando Church the sentry Daniel William Cloud was standing very still. It was strange, only a moment ago he had been pacing the platform, thinking about the path that had led him here instead of to Saint Louis, and now he was standing very still, as if there was nothing to do but look.

He could not have moved if he had wanted to. It was strange, his hands were shaking, he was trembling all over, but he could not move. He could only stare at the bare land to the west where—only a minute before—there had been nothing but empty air.

Jesus God, he murmured, and breathed it over and

over, *Jesus God ... there must be hundreds ... thousands. ...*

His head shook in automatic disbelief. *Look at them, the way the light shines. ...*

Then the air started coming back into his body and his knees were shaking. He ran for the bell rope and started pulling with all his might, pulling it again and again, as hard as he could, until the blood was pounding in his ears as the waves of warning sound spread over the flat land.

For hours that morning, and well before Dan-iel Cloud stood transfixed, staring in the bell tower, the air around the Plaza had been troubled by a strange sound. A low rumble at first, hardly more than a whisper, it had grown in intensity to a roar, until it rattled in the ears and jolted the dreams of all who heard. Those creaking wheels, cries to the oxen, that jangling of pots and pans could mean only one thing. The Mexicans of San Antonio de Béxar were leaving town.

Most of the men in the Texas Volunteer Army did not want to hear. They had gone to sleep late in the Mexi-can houses in town where they got room and board, fall-ing into bed with the haunting rhythms of the guitar still ringing in their heads. If they thought of anything at all, it was of how the sound of castanets last night had mingled with the scrape of Davy Crockett's fiddle and the genuine Scottish drone of John McGregor's bagpipes, and of how naturally the Mexicans had danced *cachuchas* while the Texans shuffled and double-shuffled and cut the pigeon's wing. It was not a good morning to get up early to investigate anything. Besides, there was not much they could do. Their horses had been put out to pasture on Salado Creek, five miles out of town.

To those who saw, the procession was both amusing and disturbing. Serapes gave it the air of a gypsy caravan. Everyone was shouting, welcoming cousins, friends, hangers-on aboard as the wheels of the ox carts, vast disks cut from giant cottonwood trunks, moved groaningly over the ruts in the road, bouncing the floor boards of wagons freighted down with furniture, bed clothing, stoves, and children. They might have been going to a fiesta as they headed out over the muddy road to the northwest, where the leading families owned *rancherias* in addition to their homes around the Plaza.

What made the movement ominous was less its racket than its size. San Antonio had, of course, been full of rumors for a long time—the bad ones usually crowding out the good—and as early as a week before scattered families had begun leaving town. But this was no trickle of refugees. Today all San Antonio seemed bent on going to the country.

It was easy to see why they were leaving, if they believed the report brought to Jim Bowie that Santa Anna and several thousand troops were on the Medina, eight miles south. Some—those families whose members were helping the Americans—had to get away. And the others, the uncommitted ones, had an equally good reason for not remaining with their Anglo-American friends. If they joined the Texans and lost, the reprisal at Mexican hands would be beyond belief. And if they joined and won, what then? What chance would they have if the Texans were not true to their word to form a Republic of Texas and joined the United States instead? There were signs of it already. Had not Travis and the War Party been getting guns and ammunition from the States for a long time? Were not most of the men at the Alamo from the States—and was it not the fear of shutting off this flow of volunteers that had sparked the present trouble? The signs were unmistakable. This Sam Houston, for example—this strange man who sometimes wore Indian clothing and went on retreats among the Indians when he felt sick at heart— what was he doing in Texas anyway? He had come four years ago for a visit; he remained as commander in chief. He had come as a friend of President Andrew Jackson; he remained, perhaps, as Jackson's spy.

No, they would not be taken in that way—not when there were Texans saying the land rightfully belonged to the States, had belonged to them ever since the Louisiana Purchase. Better to play it safe and go to the country— their own country where they had farms to tend.

The surprising thing was that any remained. On Soledad Street, within sight of the San Fernando bell tower, the Esparza boys and their little sister still played, darting in and out of the buildings and filling the street with their laughter. It had seemed strange to Daniel Cloud that they were still here, when Gregorio Esparza was known to have joined the Texan cause.

But even more surprising—to the Mexicans leaving town, at least—was not why San Antonians were leaving but why Texans were staying. Were they complete fools, to remain standing in the path of what could only cut them down? Where was there to hide in San Antonio? And what was there to protect, now that they had all their possessions with them? Why were the Anglos here at all, in a land that meant nothing to them, a land that was not even their own? They were surely greater idiots than even the Mexicans supposed if they remained now when all common sense said to flee.

Such were the questions in the Mexican mind, but before they could be answered a new sound had torn across the quiet city—the bell of San Fernando used only for the Angelus and Mass and the most solemn of occasions, pealing urgently now as they had never heard it at this time of day.

Ambrosio Rodriguez, on the road to the north where he had just said good-by to his family, heard the sound and looked up with alarm. He had told the Americans, he thought, told them time and time again. And each time Travis had said the same thing: *I know, but I would rather die here than abandon this town which is the key to Texas.*

It had been, Ambrosio Rodriguez reflected as he stared in the direction of the sound, like talking to a stone wall.

WILLIAM BARRET TRAVIS was the first man up the narrow steps of the bell tower, followed closely by Dr. John Sutherland, one of the post's six doctors. On the platform they found Cloud wildly pulling the bell rope. Travis covered his ears. Any enemy within twenty miles would be alerted by now.

As Sutherland surveyed the countryside, Travis questioned the sentry, who could hardly speak for excitement. The Mexicans had come back, he said, thousands of them.

"Where?" Dr. Sutherland asked. As more Texans swarmed onto the platform, Daniel Cloud pointed—to his surprise—to emptiness. Where only a moment before he had seen hundreds, perhaps thousands, of Mexican soldiers performing maneuvers on horseback, seen lances and pennons and glistening helmets, now there was nothing but flat, bare landscape. The semidesert land shone white in the early morning sun.

Disbelief was the easiest reaction after fear. The sentry, the men decided, had seen a mirage. Perhaps he was still drunk from last night's fandango. Cloud could only stammer out a protest. He had seen them, had even seen their lances gleaming in the sun. One of the men laughed. The greenhorn sentry had better go back to sleep. Grumbling about youngsters still wet behind the ears, the men scrambled back downstairs.

Travis and Sutherland stayed behind. Travis wanted to believe his men—he always had, trusting them more than some of them knew—but this time he could not. It was not that the sentry was lying, for the look on his face showed unmistakably that he had seen something, or thought he had. But seen what? An advance patrol that the bell had frightened away? Or had he only, like the Mexicans leaving San Antonio that morning, been panicked into seeing something that was not there?

Walking around the bell tower, Travis studied the barren, winter-stricken land that stretched in all directions far as the eye could see. Santa Anna, he told himself again, would have had to cross three hundred miles of that land, and cross it in February weather. His horses would have had to eat—and whatever Jim Bowie might say about dry mesquite grass the fact remained that much of that grass had been burned in the last campaign by Texas scouts. It was only two months since then, two months since the last Mexican soldier in Texas had crossed the Rio Grande in defeat.

It was not a thought to be taken lightly, those four straight Texas victories—at Gonzales, at Goliad, at Concepción, particularly at Béxar, where General Cós had been utterly routed after four furious days of fighting that had cost the Texans the life of Ben Milam. Cós had given up the fort he had improvised out of the near ruins of the Alamo and, surrendering to superior Texan marksmanship, had left, promising never to return. It was no small thing that the Texans, without so much as a declaration of war or independence, had driven south of the Rio Grande the last remnants of any Mexican army ever in Texas. Most of the Texans had thought the war for independence was over—thought they were free men.

But if the defeat of General Cós was not to be taken lightly, neither was the Matamoros venture that now left the Alamo weaker than the Texans stationed there liked to admit. From the first there had been those—Dr. James Grant and Colonel F. W. Johnson among others—who had wished to follow up the victory and carry the war into Mexico. Matamoros, the Mexican port south of the Rio Grande which would have been crucial in any future invasion of Texas, had been the target chosen. And "Matamoros fever," with its promise of loot and adventure, was the new ailment that had swept like wildfire through the troops.

It would have been a difficult time for the Texas Volunteer Army in any case. The larger part of the men who had fought against General Cós in the campaign of 1835 were backwoods farmers who had signed up for only two months, at a relatively convenient time between harvest and spring planting. By December most of them had been needed back at their farms. To their astonishment Travis and the other volunteers from the States suddenly found themselves the largest component of the Texas army.

For two hundred of these men then to set off from the Alamo in search of more troops to fight could only mean a weakening of the gravest sort. The fever which had already split the provisional government into two governments now split the army—and for the same reason, the thought of glory. Travis might have been a part of it himself if he had not felt it his responsibility to hold this position. Certainly there was no glory in being co-commander of a fort that was largely a crumbling ruin.

It was stronger now, of course—Jim Bowie and Major Green B. Jameson had seen to that—but Travis could have used those two hundred men. Ironically, they had not got to Matamoros at all, but were stalled at Goliad, 85 miles southeast on the San Antonio River, waiting for Colonel James W. Fannin to make up his West Point mind about whether to carry the war to the "halls of Montezuma."

The statistics were not good. Fannin had almost five hundred men. Travis had one hundred fifty. It would take a thousand to defend the Alamo.

There was no need for alarm, Travis told himself. Fannin might be on his way this very minute. Still, he wished Goliad were not several days' march away....

Frowning, he looked up to see Dr. Sutherland standing before him, waiting for an answer to a question Travis had not heard. Private Cloud, Sutherland said, still swore he had seen Mexican troops.

Travis studied the older man's face. Sutherland was an able doctor, who had healed most of the men wounded in the campaign against General Cós, and a successful businessman as well. His face showed mingled resolution and doubt.

Turning, Travis yelled to Private Cloud to remain at his post and next time to see straight. But he hurried down the stairs to call for volunteers.

THE MEN assembled in the Plaza below the bell tower of San Fernando were not accustomed to orders. Discipline was not the strong point of this army of volunteers that seldom got its pay, where every man was his own general, as well as his own quartermaster and commissary.

The sharp tone of Travis's request, asking for volunteers to ride out and look over the hill, broke rudely into their thoughts. They had considered the whole thing a joke—a stupid greenhorn's mirage—and not a good joke at that, shaking them from their beds the one morning they wanted to sleep. Some of them, pursuing their pleasure, had gone to bed only a few hours before. The Travis who stood before them now, however, left no doubts as to his seriousness. His eyes flashed with a new authority, one they had not seen before, and after the initial doubts a tremor of excitement went through the ranks. Maybe there would be some action after all. Maybe someone had finally assumed command around here.

His request, however, was clearly impossible. Even if they had felt up to walking the five miles to Salado Creek

to get their horses, there was no time for doing so. Someone with a horse would have to go. Their eyes swung to
Dr. Sutherland and John W. Smith.

John Sutherland had been in Texas only three months
now and in San Antonio only thirty days. He had come
here for the climate, not to fight. He was not an army man
at all, just as he was not originally a doctor, but an Alabama planter whose hobby of medicine had become a full-
time pursuit. And it was not freedom but the dry, healthy
air of San Antonio had caused him to come out here, following an older brother. Even now his family was waiting
in Alabama, ready to follow as soon as he gave the word.

A glance at the assembled faces put an end to his
thoughts. These were not all army men either. Many of
the younger ones had never fired a gun before except to
hunt squirrels. Silently he mounted, grateful for a horse he
could rely upon.

Travis repeated his orders, and Sutherland made a request of his own. Would Travis remind the sentry in the
tower to pull the bell rope for dear life if he saw them riding back at full speed? Travis nodded, and, with Smith at
his side, Dr. Sutherland wheeled his horse and rode away.

The men in the Plaza watched them go in silence. The
sun was higher now and they were beginning to feel their
fatigue. They wished Travis would dismiss them. Despite
his new authority, few of them really believed that old
Santy Anny and his yellow-bellies had crossed the desert
in the wintertime, and shortly they ceased to worry about
it. There were better things to fill your mind with—better
things, such as the munificent land bounties Texas was going to give them as soon as it won its independence. . . .

SUTHERLAND AND SMITH were good riders, and Smith had already proved himself a superb scout when, the previous December, he had been able to supply the Texans an invaluable map of San Antonio for their successful attack. A large part of the victory at that time had been due to his superb engineering skill.

Unlike the newcomer Sutherland, John W. Smith had been in Texas ten years, coming there from Virginia by way of Missouri in 1826. And unlike Sutherland, with his doctor's sense of detachment, John Smith felt involved with the land in a peculiar way.

He had been a married man when he came there to collect a $4,000 debt. Succumbing to the spell of the countryside, he had written his wife in Missouri to follow him. Her brothers, though, were full of stories—stories of Indians that delighted the two Smith children but froze the blood of their mother. Instead of coming, she sent word that she was getting a divorce.

It was a heavy blow for a young landowner with a resounding character endorsement from the twelve leading citizens of Hannibal in his pocket, but the young Smith liked the little town of Béxar too much to turn back. The town liked him too. His red hair got him a nickname, *"El Colorado";* his good sense got him riches. In time he met and fell in love with Maria Jesus de Curbelo, a descendant of one of the Canary Island families Philip V had sent over to help found New Spain—and in time he married her. Joining the Catholic Church, he was baptized in San Fernando and was soon making a home for himself. Already he had welcomed into it another young settler, Sam Maverick. He had become one of the three richest men in town.

It was Maria he was thinking of now as he rode over the muddy road beside Sutherland. Like other Texan leaders who had married Mexican girls—Jim Bowie, Capt. William Cooke, "Deaf" Smith, Philip Dimitt, and others— he knew the conflict as a personal one, knowing full well the struggle in his wife's mind, forced to choose between her countrymen and her Anglo-American husband—and the pride in his own when he had learned of her decision. At this very moment she was waiting on Soledad Street for the wagon he had ordered to remove her and her friends, the Esparza family, to safety.

As they rode now over the hilly trail to the west, Smith looked back with a feeling of warmth toward the town that had welcomed him and given him a home. Like an oasis it lay in the arms of the milky-green San Antonio River, flowing clear and sixty feet wide from its headspring only a few miles to the north. The town looked peaceful and clean, with its rows of adobe houses along Soledad—itself a reminder of the peaceful days when Solitary Street had been the only street in town. Now there were a number of streets in this city of four thousand people. And yet, for all the skill Don Antonio Menchaca had shown in straightening the trails so that the low, flat-roofed houses would face onto the two open plazas in the semblance of a military fort, it was hard to think of it as a place of war, a place to be defended. It had stood against the Comanches and the Lipans, but it could hardly stand against Santa Anna.

Nor did the five crumbling missions scattered along the river offer much defense. The Spaniards had usually established equally strong *presidios,* or forts, to accompany their missions, but in the case of the Alamo and the four others near San Antonio—abandoned years ago—they had for some reason failed to do so. The missions stood, useless and moldering, evidence of a once-powerful missionary zeal and a reminder of other, more peaceful, days.

Exchanging a silent glance, the two scouts rode cautiously on. The sudden shower during the night had made the road slippery and deepened its mudholes. The ruts were a snare. Looking back at San Fernando tower, the two men had a feeling of urgent eyes upon them as they sped their horses over the wet road. The temperature was at a pleasant sixty degrees, and the time was nearing noon.

WAITING FOR NEWS that would put their gnawing doubts to rest, the Texans in the Plaza had focused upon the passing caravan as a means of killing time. It disturbed them to see their companions of last night, who only a few hours ago had been grinning and comparing Davy Crockett's fiddle-and-bagpipe contest with the sound of cats in a beehive, driving their ox carts solemnly by.

To all Texan queries the Mexicans replied with evasion. "*Señor*, it is time to tend the fields." In winter? "*Señor*, it is spring! Look, already the willows are out." As if in proof, some flicked their mules with branches bearing the first spring leaves.

Travis, running his fingers through his thatch of fiery red hair, was also thinking of the early spring. He had been so sure Santa Anna could not arrive before March 15. But then he had been sure of so many things. He remembered with chagrin how he had insisted, at the defeat of General

Cós two months before, that no Mexican army would ever invade Texas again. It was frightening, the tricks time played.

If only Bonham would arrive, he kept thinking—Jim Bonham, the courier he had sent to Colonel Fannin six days before. Bonham was a distant cousin, and old friend of Travis's since they had gone to school together in Red Banks, South Carolina. If any man could talk Fannin into coming, the eloquent Bonham could.

What was needed now was time to think. Calling Davy Crockett, he placed him in command of the Plaza until he formulated his plans.

The one he dreaded to see was Bowie. He had not forgotten the parade Bowie had staged as a rebuke to him only nine days before, the parade that said Bowie too was in command here. He would be waiting now with a comment about understanding the Mexican mind, feeling superior for having adopted their ways.

Travis, on the other hand, had adopted no one's ways. He was proud of being different, different even from his own men, among whom he alone wore a regular uniform. If he had adopted Mexican ways, taking over that mentality bred for centuries on regimentation, he would have left San Antonio long ago. "To leave—it is common sense," Ambrosio Rodriguez had said, but this was not a common-sense war, as Travis was not a common-sense man. Nothing about the Texans made common-sense. Travis was proud of belonging to a people who had known no moderation from the time they fought the revolution against England to the day they followed Stephen F. Austin into this wilderness.

While Davy Crockett and the other Alamo men watched the exodus of townsfolk and shook their heads,

William B. Travis set about asking himself how to defend an entire city when you had not enough troops even to man its mission fort. . . .

SUTHERLAND AND SMITH were about a mile and a half out of town when they saw the Mexican cavalry. Reined-in at the crest of the highest western hill, they could only sit in silence, the blood draining from their faces, and stare as Private Daniel Cloud had stared earlier that morning.

Below them, in a clearing between chaparral and mesquite thicket, were fifteen hundred Mexican cavalry troops performing maneuvers in the morning sun. Again it was the glint of sunlight on the polished lances that held the scouts motionless. They had never seen anything like it—the lances dipping and flashing among the flutter of pennons, the light gleaming on hundreds of sabres. The scouts tried not to look at one another. It took only a moment to calculate that here on horseback alone was a force ten times that now waiting in the Plaza.

Nor had they ever seen such uniforms—the dragoons in their red short coats and vivid blue trousers, their high black helmets decorated with horsehair or bearskin, the men armed with lances and pennons, with sabres, with carbines and holster pistols. But if the cavalry looked elegant, their commander, riding up and down in front of his men, looked most elegant of all. In golden epaulets and red frogging, a high-peaked broad sombrero hiding his face, he waved his sword as he rode. Stately in his indigo blue jacket, his slashed trousers disappearing into the silver guards of his stirrups, General Ramirez y Sesma was surely as forbidding as Santa Anna himself would have been. Instinctively and in

spite of himself, Dr. Sutherland glanced at the buckskin
hunting shirts and trousers he and his companion wore.

The gesture reminded him of their position. Perhaps
they had been seen. At this very moment the Mexican
general might be ordering the attack. With a glance at
John W. Smith and a hasty exchange of words, Dr. Sutherland wheeled his mount. Spurring their horses violently,
they raced away in the direction of the Plaza.

As they fled downhill, John Smith's thoughts were of
his wife, waiting now for the wagon he had arranged to
send. For the first time the sense of immediate danger struck
home.

The cry behind him brought him to a halt on the slippery hill. When he turned, he saw that Sutherland was
down, struggling beneath his horse.

Smooth-shod, Dr. Sutherland's horse had been having trouble all morning. Now, spurred to a gallop in the
mud from last night's rain, it had stumbled fifty yards
below the crest of the hill and come to a stiff-legged halt
that threw the doctor to the ground and pitched his gun
from his hand. The horse, sliding, had fallen directly across
the rider's knees.

Sutherland said not a word as Smith knelt beside him.
He tried not to alarm Smith. Their message was all-impor-
tant. When he reached for the gun, after Smith had
brought both horse and rider to their feet, he found it
broken off at the breech.

Back on his horse, Sutherland knew he was badly
lamed. But his pain must not delay the message. He told his
companion to gallop ahead while there was still time.

Once within sight of San Antonio, Sutherland looked

back. If Santa Anna had seen them, he had not yet given chase.

The bell of the tower of San Fernando Church was now ringing violently, spreading the news in all directions that the two riders were returning at full speed. Daniel Cloud, with all the fury of a man whose word had been questioned, was pulling the rope triumphantly, giving the alarm to Travis, to the Mexicans leaving town, to Santa Anna himself. The louder peals told the breathless riders they were nearing home. Then, as they entered the town, the bell stopped ringing. The Plaza was deserted, white and empty in the midday sun. The houses were silent shells. On their sweating horses, Smith and Sutherland could not have known that at the first tolling peals from the bell tower Travis had given the order the men were waiting for—the order to withdraw into the Alamo.

3

The Alamo had been abandoned as a mission in 1793. Founded in 1718 by Franciscan friars as part of Spain's attempt to bring Christianity and civilization to the Indians, it had flourished long enough for the erection of a convent, whitewashed outer walls, and a large chapel, begun in 1744. Then disease had set in—disease and the strange reluctance of the Indians in Texas to accept the usually successful Spanish system. By 1793, when the friars left, only forty-three Indian converts could be found.

Physically, however, the mission was impressive. Named after the patron saint whose statue graced the front of the chapel, it was seldom called by its proper name of San Antonio de Valero, but was affectionately known as the Alamo, after *los alamos,* the cottonwood trees that lined the *acequias,* or water ditches, that flowed on its east and west sides and under its very walls. Some said the name derived from the Flying Company of the Alamo of Parras in Coahuila, a Spanish-Mexican garrison stationed there sporadically until 1825. Since 1801 it had been used continually as a military fort.

Like the four other missions that lined the San Antonio River, it was constructed in the Franciscan pattern. A large rectangular court, or plaza, of about three acres—154 yards long by 54 yards wide—was framed by stone walls 3 feet thick and from 9 to 12 feet high. Against these on three sides, facing onto the court, were small adobe rooms. The main entrance into the court, a ten-foot-wide porte-cochere, divided the strongly built stockade on the south into two parts: the fort prison, and the soldiers' quarters known as the low barracks. A stockade gate made another entrance at the point where the south wall turned inward to become a well-barricaded stockade fence. This gate, which formed the western end of the fence, was eight feet wide.

On the fourth side of the rectangle, along the eastern edge of the main enclosure, were two buildings of importance. The largest building in the Alamo, the two-story mission convent that had housed many of the Texans since they took the fort from General Cós, was known as the main barracks. Almost two hundred feet long, it had a lower floor as armory and quarters and an upper floor available as a hospital. The other building, about 50 feet to the southeast, was the original church of the mission, the chapel.

The Alamo chapel was of all the buildings in the Alamo the one in the worst state of repair. Its roof had caved in as early as 1762. Debris filled its apse and nave. No longer usable for religious services, it consisted at this time of little more than a hard earth floor and outer walls. It was, however, the strongest of the buildings, its walls reaching massively to the sky, 4 feet thick and 22 feet high. It was well-placed, behind a 4-foot-high inner wall and court. The men of the Alamo had little choice but to look to it for final refuge until reinforcements could arrive. The mission had not been built with the idea of withstanding enemy attack and siege.

By all rights the Alamo should not have been there at all. Within the last year three men had been given the responsibility of blowing it up. None had complied.

Colonel James Clinton Neill had been first. Commander of the Alamo since the departure of Colonel Johnson for Matamoros, he had been well aware of how this venture had drained away the very lifeblood of the mission fort. With only 104 discouraged men left, the Alamo could hardly stand against enemy attack. There were equally great problems about destroying it. He had not even mules and horses enough to salvage the fort's cannon.

Jim Bowie's orders, when he arrived with some thirty men on January 19, were more specific. Sam Houston, commander in chief, had become alarmed about the weakening of the Alamo and had given Bowie specific orders to blow up the mission, salvage the guns, and retreat to Goliad.

William Barret Travis arrived, bringing twenty-five men, on February 3, sent by Governor Henry Smith for the same purpose. But the issue had already been decided the previous day by Neill and Bowie. On February 2, Bowie had written Governor Smith:

The salvation of Texas depends in great measure on keeping Béxar out of the hands of the enemy. It stands on the frontier picquet guard, and if it was in the possession of Santa Anna, there is no stronghold from which to repel him in his march to the Sabine. Colonel Neill and myself have come to the solemn resolution that we will rather die in these ditches than give them up to the enemy.

It was a decision in which Travis, who felt he had loosed Santa Anna's revenge, could only concur. By doing so he disobeyed his governor, as Bowie disobeyed his commander in chief, and as Neill—soon to leave because of illness in the family—disobeyed both. But the Alamo was still standing on the afternoon of February 23, when Travis ordered his men inside.

IT WAS THE TEXANS' first and only retreat, and they executed it in an orderly manner. Leaving Davy Crockett in the square to await the return of the scouts, Travis issued the necessary orders to move his men across the river and to the fort, a half-mile east of town. There was no question of holding San Antonio. The mission itself would be hard enough to hold.

As the men moved along Protero Street, the women of the town, weeping openly, watched them pass. Some were heard to exclaim, "You will all be killed." What would they do now that the Texans were leaving?

The troops themselves were in good spirits. True, discipline had not been a strong point with them; they were unused to being assigned duties. But now that the moment was at hand they could rise to it. If Santa Anna wanted a fight, he would have a fight—and about time too! It reminded them of Davy Crockett's statement on arriving at the Alamo with his Tennessee boys two weeks before: "We heard you were having trouble with the likes of old

Santy Anny and we 'lowed as how we might help you, since we like a good fight." The attitude had so cheered the Anglos that they celebrated it that night with a fandango, and had been celebrating ever since. Now they had had enough of fandangos. This was business, and they would show they could follow orders as well as the next man. Travis was in command now—Travis and Jim Bowie.

One Texan—Capt. Almeron Dickinson of the Texas artillery—felt a personal alarm. He and his eighteen-year-old wife and their fifteen-month-old daughter had living quarters just a short way from the Plaza, at the bougain-villea-vined stone house of the Ramón Músquiz family. Mrs. Dickinson had become a great friend of Señora Músquiz, whose husband was the *jefe político*, or deputy governor, at Béxar.

Not long after the bells stopped clanging, the frightened ladies at the door of the Músquiz house saw Captain Dickinson flagging his horse down the street. He filled the landscape. Mrs. Dickinson had her baby in her arms. Her husband galloped up, reined his mount to a swift stop, and landed on the ground sooner than his horse's front legs. For a second words would not come. Then Captain Dickinson leaped toward the *portal*. "Quick, Sue," he exclaimed, "the Mexicans are upon us! Give me the babe and jump on behind me!" Without a word she handed the child to him, after he had leaped back into the saddle. He kicked the stirrup free for her left foot, stretched an arm out to her, and she pulled herself by the pommel on to the saddle blanket behind him. Holding onto him with one hand, she took the baby into her free arm. With a long look and a shake of her head, she made a helpless gesture of farewell to Señora Músquiz.

Fearing the Mexican army might be already entering town, the Dickinsons galloped across the river at the ford south of the Alamo and entered the fort at its southern gate. There were several other women inside—wives or relatives of San Antonians who were fighting with the Texans —but Mrs. Dickinson was the only woman there from the States.

Enrique Esparza and his mother entered the Alamo shortly behind the Dickinsons, with but one difference: the Dickinsons had seen advance outposts, but the twelve-year-old Mexican boy had seen Santa Anna. . . .

AS DR. SUTHERLAND and John Smith, led by Davy Crockett, approached the Alamo, they noted the remarkable change that had taken place since they left only a few hours before. The mission fortress had come alive with energy and purpose. Cannons were being readied; on the walls men could be seen passing a telescope from hand to hand. Jim Bowie, a yelling, noisy giant, was everywhere at once directing the erection of platforms. Only Travis, busy drafting messages, was nowhere in sight.

Bristling with their news, the scouts yet took time to observe the activity as they entered the courtyard. Everywhere men were making ready rapidly and with skill, reinforcing the outside rampart walls with earth mounds, breaking apart old horseshoes for cannon shot, checking on food and water and supplies. The Alamo had a good water supply, because of the *acequias* built by the missionaries to sluice off the flow from the San Antonio to irrigate their corn and beans. Despite these ditches, however, one of which flowed directly through the Alamo's courtyard, it was clear that a well inside the walls was essential in case the enemy tried to shut off the flow of water. So near were they to the headsprings of the San Antonio, a source had already been struck.

In front of the chapel a dozen men were busy molding bullets from little leaden filigree ornaments that had decorated the window casings of the old Alamo chapel. Flintlocks were being made ready with all their accouterment: wiping stick, ramrod, powder horn, bullet pouch. At the walls an Irish captain named Danny Ward was solemnly preparing his defense. It was the first time Dr. Sutherland had seen him completely sober in a long time.

Attempting to dismount, Dr. Sutherland discovered he could not stand. Travis, coming from his headquarters room on the lower floor of the stone-walled, two-storied barracks, heard Sutherland's report on the position of the Mexican cavalry. He asked the doctor if he could walk.

Sutherland shook his head. He was only good on horseback, he explained. He could still ride a horse as well as any man.

Travis nodded, his thoughts elsewhere. There was immediate necessity for sending messengers to Gonzales, to Goliad, to Washington-on-the-Brazos and the constitutional convention about to get under way there. The people in the States should be notified. The whole nation must be aroused.

"Do you think you can make it to Gonzales?" Travis asked Sutherland. The doctor nodded. "I want you to go to Gonzales," Travis continued, "and rally the settlers to our relief."

Returning to his table while Smith went to look after his wife, Travis quickly wrote out messages for Gonzales and Goliad. These were his nearest and most probable sources. There would be time later for more organized reports and other couriers.

His first message was to Andrew Ponton, *alcalde* or mayor, of Gonzales. After noting that the enemy was already in sight, Travis wrote:

> We want men and provisions. Send them to us. We have 150 men and are determined to defend the Alamo to the last. Send an express to San Felipe with news night and day.—TRAVIS

Handing the message to Sutherland, Travis told him to inform the outside world he would fire three cannon shots each day—at dawn, at noon, and at sunset—to show they were still alive in the Alamo.

Dr. Sutherland gave him a last look. Then, spurring his horse, he set off to rejoin Smith. The two couriers had gone only a short way before they heard cannon fire behind them and, up ahead, saw Jim Bonham returning, a solitary figure on the uninhabited Gonzales road.

AT THE AGE of twenty-eight James Butler Bonham met life with defiance. In college in South Carolina he had defied the entire school administration, with near-tragic results. As a young lawyer in South Carolina, he had once offered to tweak a judge's nose. It made him all the more indignant now to be returning with bad news. With all his powers of eloquence he had been unable to persuade Colonel Fannin to bring his troops to Béxar.

It was not Bonham's fault, nor even Fannin's. But Bonham was determined to find where the fault lay. An army so split that one section could not aid another; a government whose leaders were all away; and now a ridiculous struggle for power in Sam Houston's army. Three different men—Dr. James Grant, Colonel F. W. Johnson, and Fannin himself—all claiming to be in command. Just thinking of it was enough to bring an angry flush to Bonham's face as he hailed the Alamo scouts.

Bonham's news was bad, but nothing compared with what he now heard from Sutherland and Smith. Hurriedly he pressed for details. What was the enemy strength? What was the cannon firing they had just heard? On the latter point the couriers were as mystified as he. They had taken the Goliad road to avoid being seen by the Mexican cavalry, then swung east toward Gonzales, but no enemy had been that near the Alamo when they left. It was not noon, nor was it sunset, but three in the afternoon. It could not be Travis's signal.

"I must get to Travis," Bonham said.

Dr. Sutherland suggested he might better help spread word of Travis's plight. It might be dangerous going back. He could not keep the suspicion out of his voice, that Travis, in sending Bonham to Fannin the very day he had officially protested Bowie's drunkenness, had had an additional motive beyond securing reinforcements. Perhaps he had even offered to exchange commands or somehow get rid of Bowie.

Bonham had no intention of revealing his mission. He was going into the Alamo, he announced, and all Santa Anna's forces would have a hard time keeping him out.

Waving good-by to the couriers, he pulled himself high in his stirrups, lashed his horse with his reins, and spurred the animal to a gallop, straight ahead into the fortress unmolested. When Jim Bonham rode through the Alamo gate, which a dozen eager hands swung open for him, he learned the meaning of the cannon fire he had heard on the Gonzales road. It was primarily meant to startle Santa Anna. It was Travis's reply to a demand of surrender.

THE ANSWERS to the questions Jim Bonham had been asking himself on the Goliad road were many and complex. Basically they went back to Christmas and the Matamoros Expedition and the freedom in the Texas Volunteer Army.

It had started with Dr. James Grant, a Scottish doctor, and his extensive holdings of land in Texas and Northern Mexico. In Texas he held millions of acres; in Mexico, at Parras, he had even more extensive holdings until pushed out by Santa Anna's dictatorial regime. The only way to recover his property was to persuade Colonel Johnson, and after him the commander at Goliad, Colonel Fannin, to carry the war south. They had just given General Cós a glorious defeat. They could hardly stop there and give him a chance to rebuild his forces. The split over this tactic that resulted in the two-month-old provisional government of Governor Henry Smith was still, in February, 1836, as far as ever from being healed.

They had long been at odds—the impatient, fighting-mad Smith of the War Party and his more cautious advisers in the general council. With the fresh impetus of the Matamoros Expedition, each denounced the other. Smith violently refused to cooperate, as the Council wished, with such liberal Mexican leaders as General Mexia, Captain Miracle, and ex-ambassador Lorenzo de Zavala. The council impeached Smith as a warmonger and set up Lieutenant-

Governor James Robinson as acting governor; but Smith, who had fought hard in the skirmishes of 1832 and could fight again, refused to be impeached. Carrying on as a one-man government, he threatened to shoot any councilman who tried to seize the state seal.

The situation in the army was even more confused, largely because of the absence of Sam Houston. Houston, ruling the regulars but not volunteers, had known for some time of Santa Anna's attempts to incite the Indians to raid the settlements in advance of the impending war which Mexico expected to win. Fuming now at the frustrations of a divided government but loyal to Smith, Houston decided it would be a good time to make sure that the Indians in East Texas stayed out of the war. Relinquishing command, he took a furlough until March 1, when a new meeting of the Texas Constitutional Convention was to be held. Until that body met and granted him absolute authority over all forces, the one whom the Indians called alternatively "The Raven" and "Big Drunk" would be in East Texas making treaties with his friends, the Cherokees. He thought, and rightly, that Fannin, Grant, and Johnson had conspired with the Council to steal his power away from him. He was a commander-in-chief without an army.

Stephen F. Austin, meanwhile, was traveling toward Washington attempting as ambassador to secure men and money from the United States. With two others, he had set out the day after Christmas to negotiate a loan of a million dollars, fit out a navy, get army enlistments, and find out Washington's attitude toward annexation. By February 12 he had got no farther than Nashville. He was detained there by unseasonable cold and ice. The result was that the two strongest men in Texas history, Austin and

Houston, were either out of the country or away from the crucial action at its most critical moment, leaving a wide-open field to those who remained behind.

The contested claims to leadership were not long in coming. Colonel Francis W. Johnson had been named commander in chief of volunteers by the previous commander, Colonel Edward Burleson, before he retired, and this authority was ratified by his general council. Colonel Fannin claimed, correctly, that the council had reversed itself and conferred the authority upon him. Dr. Grant and Colonel Johnson worked as a team, and Johnson shared command with the magnetic Scot.

As commander at Goliad, however, where the main concentration of Texas troops was, Colonel Fannin had the advantage. For all practical purposes he was now commander in Texas, and all Sam Houston could do about it was send Jim Bowie to the Alamo to blow it up, as Governor Henry Smith had independently sent William B. Travis.

It was no wonder that Colonel James Fannin, sitting in his headquarters room at Goliad studying the toes of his well-polished boots, felt a sense of satisfaction with the decision he had made. It was not, after all, the ex-West Pointer reminded himself, as if the Alamo had already been fired upon, or as if it constituted the main part of Texas strength. The Alamo should have been blown up long ago. Both Bowie and Travis had had their opportunity, and they had refused to obey.

GENERAL ANTONIO LOPEZ DE SANTA ANNA had prepared his entrance into Texas psychologically at the Rio Grande. At

Laredo, where he had been a guest at a fancy ball staged in his honor, he had issued decrees about the punishment in store for the Texans. He would execute, he said, all leaders of the revolution, confiscate Texan property to pay for the expenses of war, drive all participants in the uprising from the province, remove all nonparticipants into the interior of Mexico, treat as pirates and execute any Americans who had come into Texas as part of the volunteer armed forces, and, finally, liberate all slaves while forbidding future settlement to all Anglo-Saxons. Now, poised on the heights overlooking San Antonio and surrounded by his impressive cortege of smartly outfitted officers, he was ready to carry out the decrees.

Beside him at Campo Santo, the cemetery where he had ordered a halt while a salute was fired and details under Colonel Miñon scoured the town for information, was his personal aide, Colonel Juan Almonte. For this campaign Santa Anna had left behind his French military expert, Jean Garat, who fed him Napoleonic lore and legend, and who had secured for him an impressive collection of Napoleonic mementos. There was no time, the dictator had decided, for talk of European battles on this trip or the fingering of old trophies. Those were better off in his magnificent hacienda, *Manga de Clavo*, "Spike of Clove," in Jalapa. This time he had something better to amuse himself with—his prized collection of fighting cocks. If they failed to amuse him, there was always the city of San Antonio, with which he wanted to settle an old feud.

Both Almonte and Santa Anna had been in San Antonio before, but for vastly different reasons. In 1834 the remarkable young aide had toured Texas on a presidential errand, ostensibly to reassure the settlers and canvass their needs, secretly to gauge their strength, their vulnerability to attack, their possessions, and their mood. He was an ideal choice. From his education in the States, he knew English perfectly; further, he was a man of great charm, one who could persuade the Texans he was their friend. Indeed, he had been enthusiastic about them, stressing in his report how the Texans in fifteen years of colonization, had made the soil flourish. But perhaps, with 30,000 to 40,000 settlers, they were becoming too strong. He suggested the Mexican government take proper notice of this wealthy land and colonize it to meet Anglo-American dominance, the same recommendations that had been made as early as 1829 by General Mier y Terán and that had resulted in the oppressive law of April 6, 1830, obstructing Anglo-American infiltration. First welcomed as a buffer against the Indians, the Anglos were now feared as upstart independents.

Santa Anna's first visit had been more grim. In 1813, as a youth of nineteen serving his military apprenticeship in the Royal Spanish Army, he had come to San Antonio with General Arredondo to crush a rebel army trying to establish a Republic of Texas as a part of Hidalgo's revolution for Mexico's liberation from Spain. Santa Anna had been a good pupil, had learned well from the general how to conduct war as a school of cruelty. Twenty-three years later he was back. It was the second time he had had to crush a rebellion in this town that shared his saint's name. He had reached its outskirts on his forty-second birthday.

Reaching for his Napoleonic snuffbox, the general studied the town before him. It had changed very little. The long, low Governor's Palace, symbol of Spanish dominion, still stood across from the church, bearing over its entrance the escutcheon of the regal Hapsburgs. On Soledad Street was still the one-room building where General Arredondo had forced the captive women of the community to make tortillas and tamales for his men. Santa Anna's eyes brightened at the memory.

It had been an August day of atrocious heat. Forming his 2,000 men into a U-shaped ambush outside the town of San Antonio de Béxar, Arredondo had sent out a skirmish squad and suctioned into the ambush cross-fire 2,500 rebel troops. What Santa Anna remembered most was how they had run—the Indians first, then the Mexicans, then the 850 Anglo-Americans. What did it matter if the Anglos had run only after being deserted by their allies, or if they were border ruffians and adventurers—largely pirates recruited from the domains of Jean Lafitte and the Neutral Ground, that lawless territory in dispute since the Louisiana Purchase? They were still Americans—and they had run. They deserved the death they got, as did the 327 Béxar citizens Arredondo had also killed. Ninety-three American fighters escaped. It was a loss, but a small one.

It had been Santa Anna's first large battle and his first encounter with Anglo-Americans; he had never forgotten it. Never would he forget the contempt he had felt for the Anglo-Saxons on that occasion. As a young lieutenant leading troops from Vera Cruz, he had been cited for conspicuous valor and been given a chance to share in the plunder. It had been the first of a long line of successes, and he had accepted it with the same ease with which—in 1821 and the triumph of the splinter revolts of which the Texas rebellion had been a part—he had moved over to the other side, only to reverse himself again, ten years later, in favor of dictatorship. It was all part of his pattern—to follow success and capitalize upon it—and it was not difficult if one knew which would be the successful side.

Only at the gambling table was his luck bad, and it was here that San Antonio had left an unforgivable mark on his record. The very memory of it brought rage to Santa Anna's face. He had started playing for big stakes with his newly plundered wealth. He had lost badly, and finally, in desperation, had resorted to forging a sizable note with his commander's signature. Nothing would have happened if the occupation army had not been bored in their useless town. Except for Béxar the whole thing might have been overlooked. But the men were bored, and treated the discovery of the forgery as if it were the greatest moment in Mexican history. Santa Anna had had a good explanation, claiming it involved the honor of a fellow officer whom he had saved from ignominy. He had even had money to cover the forgery, advanced by the expedition's surgeon. Unfortunately the surgeon had wanted his money back. The whole town of Béxar had joined in the amusement.

This was what he could never forget—that they had laughed at him—at him who had been cited for conspicuous valor and stood always in the line of the great *conquistadores*. Even now, after he had defeated the best soldiers in the world, those of Spain, and could push directly to Washington, D.C., if he chose, he could still see their faces distorted by laughter. It was a score he would settle, and in his own way. . . .

Santa Anna called for his horse. It was time to make a triumphal entrance into this city toward which he held an unspeakable rage.

4

Enrique Esparza, son of Gregorio Esparza, was playing in the street with his two brothers and sister when he saw General Santa Anna. Despite his mother's pleas, the twelve-year-old boy inched closer for a better look. His mother was worried because the wagon John W. Smith was to have sent had not yet arrived.

As Enrique watched, the Plaza seemed to overflow with red and blue uniforms, flying pennons, and glittering sabres. What caught his eye, however, was the Generalissimo himself, magnificent in red braid, dismounting at the old *presidio* on the northwest corner opposite the church as the bands played. He was one of the tallest of his countrymen Enrique had ever seen. The boy particularly noticed the splendid flourish with which the general handed the reins to an aide. The men at the Alamo always hitched their mounts themselves. Enrique thought it must be wonderful to be a general and hand one's reins to a subordinate.

The next few hours were filled with activity—the rush to the Alamo beside his mother, the discovery that the gates were locked. Enrique's mother pounded furiously against the doors. At last a sentry on top the chapel walls saw them, and the boy felt himself being drawn through a small window. As he climbed down beside his father over some unplaced small cannon, he heard the firing begin. It was all a wonderful game.

Drawing him to her, Gregorio Esparza's wife looked at her son who was twelve but was so small he looked only eight. In a low voice she told him he must forget all that he had seen.

But Enrique Esparza had no wish to forget. He would remember the sight of *El Presidente* until the day he died. . . .

Meanwhile Jim Bowie, at the southwest corner of the outer wall, kept a lookout. He trained his glasses in the direction of the Mexican advance, preparing his little surprise.

GENERAL ANTONIO LOPEZ DE SANTA ANNA had come to Béxar under the worst of winter conditions. He had lost men and supplies along the way, with fifty yokes of oxen frozen. He had been plagued with dysentery. Now, training his field glasses on the Alamo, he confronted the worst insult of all. Fluttering in the north wind was a Mexican flag, its large black numerals clearly visible on the middle white field: "1824." "Traitors," he fumed, "barbarians and infidels!"

For the Mexican dictator it was an unforgivable rebuke, more so than a rebel Texas flag in its place. There could be only one reason for flying it: to remind him of the constitution of 1824. It was not a subject of which he wished to be reminded.

The constitution of 1824, under which many of the Anglo-Americans had come to Texas, was one guaranteeing settlers' rights, while it held out the hope of separate statehood when sufficient population had been achieved. Santa Anna, upon coming to power, had scrapped this constitution at the same time he dissolved the state legislatures. The flying of the red, white, and green flag of the Mexican republic now was the Texans' way of saying that Santa Anna—rather than Texas—was unconstitutional. Their own position was clear: they were remaining loyal to the original agreement. They had not yet declared war. But they meant to defend their rights, by arms.

Santa Anna was enraged. These usurpers had driven out his garrisons, refused to pay duties, captured the only Mexican town of any size in the territory. Now they demanded the restoration of a different government. These, then, were the "settlers" from whom his cowardly brother-in-law had run. He had done right to give Cós so severe a tongue lashing. For people of this sort there was only one answer—the path of terrorism.

Imperiously, he gave three commands. He ordered the red flag signifying no quarter placed on San Fernando tower. He ordered a savage burst of cannon fire. And he ordered the white pennant raised to signal for a parley. It was going to be a quick surrender, faster even than the cowardly surrender in 1813. His Creole blood quickened.

He had not long to wait. The Texans responded to

all three signals with the loudest noise yet. They had an eighteen-pounder, firing missiles heavier by eight pounds than any thing Santa Anna had been able to transport. They fired it now, and the air over the Alamo was alive with Texas cheers.

It was a sound Santa Anna could not tolerate, but before he could act a further remarkable sight held him motionless. From the Alamo, simultaneously with the burst from the eighteen-pounder, emerged an Anglo-American officer bearing a white flag. It was Jim Bowie's little surprise—his reminder to Colonel Travis that they were both still in command here. The officer was Major Green B. Jameson, and the message, written by Jim Bowie in Spanish, wanted to know if it was true that a parley had been called by the Mexican side.

TRAVIS HAD NOT been informed of this move of Bowie's. Seeing Jameson now proceed to the enemy lines, he flew into a rage. In his own mind he had decided long ago that he would never surrender or retreat. What did Bowie mean now by this craven gesture? Was the Mexican-lover trying to trade out?

Nothing could have been farther from Jim Bowie's mind, and no one but Travis could have suspected him of it. He had wanted to find out what Santa Anna meant by flying the white flag. He knew the Mexican mentality; Travis denied its existence. In this case, however, Bowie found his position increasingly hard to defend. Santa Anna directed Almonte to receive "Benito" Jameson, as Bowie had named him for the occasion, and to assume that the Texans rather than the Mexicans had initiated the parley.

Had Santa Anna really raised a white flag? The dictator had no recollection of it. Jameson returned with a message worded by Almonte and Colonel Batres to make it sound like a reply to an offer of surrender on terms. The only conditions for surrender, it read, would be unconditional surrender at Santa Anna's discretion.

Jameson's return justified Travis's conviction. Bowie had made the Texans look craven. He had insulted them. Still Travis's anger would not subside. Assembling Captain Seguin and all the other men, he cut his wrath on their minds in an inspired harangue the power of which—if not the wording—was unforgettable. The Mexican cannon continued to boom, but, without adequate batteries yet erected, their purpose was to noise forth defiance and terror. When Travis had finally exhausted his anger, he administered to his men an oath of "never surrender."

Then he dismissed them, after exacting a pledge that they would resist to the end.

It was a defeat for Jim Bowie. In the battle for command, power had for the first time swung to the side of Travis. From now on, the volunteers would be testing his strength against Bowie's. Travis had begun to look like a leader.

The men rushed to the walls to see what the Mexicans were doing.

THE MEAGER SHADOWS of the winter afternoon were beginning to darken the walls at the close of the first day. Guns still cracked and occasional splinterings of stone wall or wood echoed the whine of flying bullets, but the smoke from the Alamo fires now mingled with that from the campfires of the *soldaderas* of Santa Anna's army, and the good smell of broiling meat made the men breathe deep and feel that life was purposive again. Lighting smokes from the coals of the fire, they relaxed for the first time that day.

The explosive tempers of Travis and Santa Anna had provided most of the drama of the first day of the siege. Except for one Texan horse, wounded early in the afternoon by the shot and shell the Mexicans intermittently fired into the fort, Dr. Sutherland's knee was the only Texan casualty.

The Mexicans had lost one man. Davy Crockett, spurred on by the reckless curiosity that seized all the men, had led the Texans up the ramps to the top of the walls for a quick estimate of enemy strength. Their guns were primed and ready as they hoarsely yelled at the enemy and shouted to one another, "Look at 'em run, look at those greasers run!" In premature exhilaration they tossed their coonskin caps in the air and did jigs on the improvised gun scaffolds.

The same curiosity had perhaps tempted one Mexican soldier following the river's broad looping toward the Alamo's west wall. It was here that the stream suddenly made a bend like a rattlesnake writhing with a belly ache—or so Davy Crockett had just described it, to the hilarity of his boys.

Their chuckles stopped short at the crack of Davy's gun. He had just brought down the first Mexican casualty of the encounter. It gave the Mexicans a warning about Texas marksmanship. "Ain't gonna be the last of 'em blowed to hell," muttered a Texan as he ducked the first shower of enemy musket fire.

This prelude of scattered shots now turned into a

steady bombardment. Under cover of darkness, the Mexicans started setting up batteries. On the west side of the river, four hundred yards from the Alamo, Santa Anna's men established two positions, their batteries bearing on the west and southwest walls of the fort, walls about twelve feet high and a yard thick. The guns were light, five- and nine-inch howitzers and eight-pounder cannon, for the Mexican army was not equipped with heavy siege artillery. No defenses or obstructions on this side of the fort lay between these light guns and the Alamo. The immediate damage was slight, but the roar and the menace they announced compelled the Texans to sleep right at their posts.

They had been fortunate in finding food for the siege. When they had come into the Alamo that noon, they had had only three bushels of corn. Shortly they found some twenty or thirty head of beeves roaming the deserted streets. Shouting to one another, the men drove the beeves through the gates and into the stock pens on the east side of the mission. This good luck was matched by more. Making sallies outside the walls, the foraging Texans found in the deserted Mexican huts, or *jacales,* eighty or ninety bushels of abandoned corn. They got back inside the mission walls without a scratch but with the certainty of enough corn bread to last a month.

Perhaps, Travis thought, as he stopped now a moment near the wall of the south court, the Lord had been on their side that day. Wearily he leaned against the stones of the south wall. They had saved, those stones, the Texans from spilling any blood this first day. Travis suddenly remembered a story he had heard about them.

Long ago, it was said, cows' milk and goats' milk had been mixed with the mortar for the stones of the Alamo buildings, and outer walls. Mexican mothers had kept their children on short rations so that these chapels offered to God's glory might be pure, white-gleaming, in the sharp sun. Sacrifice had been second nature to these women of the Mediterranean mold. Now it was the turn of the Texans to cement the stones of the Alamo with their sacrifice. Not the first day, nor the next, but on some day not far hence they would add to the milk-fixed mortar the red of their own blood. What day? Travis wondered. And in what amount?

The thought of these men who had come here from Alabama, from Ohio, from Scotland and Wales, and all for different reasons, suddenly overwhelmed the twenty-seven-year-old leader. He no longer felt angry. He felt tired. Even toward Bowie, whose motives he had perhaps misjudged that day, he had a new feeling of warmth.

Why had these men come here? Why was Bowie here? Why was Daniel Cloud? Was it some force that had directed them hither, for reasons they could not yet understand?

But mostly he was thinking of his own arrival—of the inescapable barrier that separated him from Bowie and all the others. For they had come to Texas for peaceable reasons. And Travis, it was said, had come because a citizen in Claiborne, Alabama, had been murdered.

THE STORY had its beginning in 1828, when Travis was nineteen years old and had been working in Claiborne in the law office of the Honorable James Dellett. Dellett, one of Alabama's leading citizens, got the young law student a job teaching school part time, to support him during his legal apprenticeship. One of his students was Rosanna Cato, the sixteen-year-old daughter of a prosperous farming family. On October 20, 1828, they were married. Travis wrote in the family Bible: "Married—on the evening of the 20th day of October A. D. 1828 William B. Travis, to Rosanna E. Cato." The following year he made the entry: "Born on the 8th day of August 1829, Charles Edward Travis, son of William B. Travis and Rosanna E. Travis." It was the last entry he made. He was twenty years old.

Less than two years later, in the early spring of 1831, the town of Claiborne was rocked by the news of a mystifying murder. Early one morning a Negro slave of Judge Dellett, working in the garden of the Dellett plantation, looked through the gate that opened onto a small racetrack the community used, and was startled to see the form lying there. When he saw the pool of blood, he realized he was looking at the body of a dead man.

Appalled, the Negro raced back to the house to tell his master. The Dellett family recognized the corpse as that of a well-known Claiborne citizen. The news spread rapidly. By noon the Alabama townspeople were persuaded that the one who found the body had also committed the murder. A formal charge was lodged against Judge Dellett's slave.

The Negro was fortunate in the counsel Judge Dellett appointed for him. The judge chose the brilliant young man whose career he had shaped—William Barret Travis.

But all Travis's skill was of no avail. As the trial came to its conclusion one late afternoon, it was obvious Travis had lost his case. The jury returned a verdict of guilty, and condemned the Negro to death by hanging.

Whatever skill Travis had shown earlier was nothing

to his now impassioned speech as he pleaded with the judge for a stay of execution and a retrial. Judge Dellett was firm. Nothing in the evidence, he said, would justify his granting Travis's request. But Travis argued so persistently that at last the judge agreed to take the matter into consideration for twenty-four hours. The young lawyer had guaranteed, with compelling sincerity, that by the next morning he could supply irrefutable proof of his client's innocence.

Late that night, after the townspeople had gone to bed, Judge Dellett had a visitor. William Barret Travis had come to talk to him, and the two men—master and disciple —talked long into the night.

Travis explained why he knew he could clear his client of the charge. It was simple. "I did it myself."

"I know," replied the judge, and asked the young lawyer why.

Travis answered that the dead man had tried to trifle with his wife.

For a long time, as Travis explained, he had never thought the jury would find the Negro guilty. The judge sat looking at the young husband with the nearly ungovernable temper. At last, when silence filled the room again, he told him he had three choices. He could do what any white man perhaps could have been expected to do: keep his mouth shut. He could confess. Or he could leave for Texas.

That same morning before it was light, William B. Travis, leaving his young wife and two-year-old son in Claiborne, got on his horse, swam him across the river, and set out for Texas from Alabama. He was never to return.

MANY ANOTHER MAN the evening of the first day wondered what he was doing at the Alamo. Many another thought of the strange turns of fate that had created this situation rather than some other.

There was the Alamo itself, that should not have been standing at all. There was Colonel Neill, who but for the sudden illness in his family two weeks ago would still have been in charge. Jim Bowie and William B. Travis had come to blow up the Alamo and had found themselves, surprisingly, its co-commanders. There was Dr. Sutherland, now removed from the scene of the Alamo by the circumstance of having been sent on a mission to Gonzales.

The Mexican army, too, by all rights should not have been there. It had been a near-impossible feat for its Generalissimo to transport the 1,800 pack mules, 300 two-wheel carts, fifty or more four-wheel wagons, the thousands of troops with their women and children and camp followers, and all their supplies, across the norther-stricken, barren semidesert in the month of February. And even here, once arrived, it might have been wiser, as some of Santa Anna's generals urged, to bypass San Antonio in favor of a direct attack on the chief settlement at San Felipe de Austin. But the same fate that held Bowie and Travis there had made the recovery of San Antonio by Santa Anna a point of honor.

At the Alamo, then, the enemies faced each other. Every advantage lay with the Mexican side. Their commanders, only two of whom had been born in Mexico, were brilliant. They outnumbered the total troops in Texas by six to one; they outnumbered the men at the Alamo by twenty to one. Most important, they were united in both organization and the habits of a lifetime. One authority prevailed, whether in Santa Anna's complete command of the army or in the Mexican impulse toward conformity in their military code or religious worship. Centuries of a master-slave society had done their work well.

The Texans, on the other hand, were divided not only in military command and in their provisional government, but in their temperaments. Stephen F. Austin was a virtuoso diplomat whose acts were determined by the sanctity of contract. Sam Houston, full of subtle craftiness, kept, as he said, his own counsel and conferred with no man. Jim Bowie explained his career in terms of a society where every man was his own law. William Barret Travis had a code, but his own, and he expected everyone to live up to it. Davy Crockett was a wanderer, looking for challenges for his extraordinary energy. Fannin, Johnson, Grant—all struggled with their private ambitions in the battle between Governor Smith and his fifteen-member council.

In military training the Texans, though they could match the skill of the Mexican conscripts in the ranks, could hardly compare with the well-trained cavalry and artillery battalions under Santa Anna. Houston and Crockett had fought Indian wars. Fannin had trained briefly at West Point. Travis and Bonham had joined their state militias. But in organized warfare the total experience of the Texans, except for that of Houston and Crockett, was almost nonexistent.

Outnumbered, divided, untrained, the Texans that night had to admit that the Mexicans had every advantage but one, and what that one was they could not quite say. It was a vague stirring somewhere—a restless feeling that they had capabilities within them of which they had never dreamed.

Daniel William Cloud felt it that night as he climbed an earthen ramp to look at the west again, to see again from the scaffold by the western wall the place where he had glimpsed 1,500 Mexican troops and their lances atop the Alazan Heights that morning. He had a feeling, vaguely within him—something about San Antonio de Béxar, the way he felt toward that town—but he could not have put it into words. He could only stand on top the scaffold looking at the blood-red wash against the horizon filtering through the filigree branches of the trees. He ducked his coonskin cap at the report of a rifle but he felt confident. In a few weeks the bluebonnets would enamel the stony soil above the Mexican army's graves.

Jim Bowie, taking a long drink by the side of a broiled beef from which he cut crusty strips with his knife, never guessed that at that moment fate was reaching out in the dark to lay a cold hand on his shoulder.

Jim Bowie was a complex man. In 1828, when
he came to Texas at the age of thirty-four in search of
silver mines, he already knew the luxury of New Orleans
and Natchez, the enchantment of the Louisiana bayous
where he grew up. He had been successful and enterprising
in the slave trade, in the operation of a saw mill, in giving
Louisiana its first steam-operated sugar press. But in his
relationship to nature he was simple, driven by a single
urge—to cover the face of the earth on horseback, to be
forever wandering, forever riding in pursuit of wealth,
in search of lost mines, riding to Nacogdoches, to Louisiana,
to Mississippi—anywhere that he might find land and find
gold: he was hungry for both. When he arrived in Texas
he was six feet one, had auburn hair, weighed 180 pounds,
and had already been in the famous fight that fixed forever

in the frontier mind his reputation as a fighter and the equally great reputation of his blade.

The fame of the Bowie knife was born, it was said, on a sandbar in the Mississippi River in 1826, when twice in a number of seconds it saved Jim Bowie's life. Bowie had come up from Louisiana, as had the dozen other participants, to witness a duel between Samuel Wells and Dr. Thomas Maddox. These two gentlemen, content to satisfy honor, fired harmless shots into the air, then exchanged handshakes across the peaceful chasm into which one of them should have fallen. Or so felt the men who had traveled far to see the real thing. First there was muttered disapproval, then a general melee. These men had not come to see honor satisfied but for excitement. They got it. When the smoke of the second battle cleared, there were two dead and two wounded. Jim Bowie was one of the wounded. The two dead had been harvested by the Bowie knife.

Bowie had been serving as second to General Cuny, who had challenged a leader of the other side, Colonel Crain. Crain, treacherously, whipped out two pistols and discharged them simultaneously. General Cuny was killed, Bowie was wounded. Colonel Crain turned and ran. The only weapon Bowie had was his knife; he drew it, straightened up, and was starting in pursuit when he fell. Before he could rise, Major Wright—a longtime enemy—rushed to try to stab him with a sword cane. With his left hand Bowie caught the cane and pulled Wright toward him. Then with a herculean plunge he cut through Wright's abdomen to his backbone. Bowie, sitting on the ground, was momentarily blinded by the blood of his victim. But he was not yet through with sword canes. Alfred Blanchard, friend of the expiring Major Wright, lunged at Bowie with a cane, his only weapon. But he reckoned without Bowie's reach or his quickness of movement. Swerving aside, Bowie swept his knife in a tremendous arc again, and slashed Blanchard crosswise in the stomach. No one else bothered him.

When Bowie recovered, he wanted to honor that blade. He had it polished, set into an ivory handle mounted with silver, its scabbard mounted with silver too. A year or so later when he was again in Texas he asked the famed Texan blacksmith, Noah Smithwick, to make a duplicate of it. He told Smithwick he did not want "to degrade this knife by ordinary use." It was not an ordinary knife nor were Bowie's fights ordinary fights.

The story of Bowie's fighting courage had become a legend even in his own lifetime. Everyone knew the stories —how he had survived fierce fights with his wrist bound to that of his opponent, fights so close that the adversaries gripped opposite ends of a handkerchief between their teeth; how on one occasion he had won a sit-down knife duel in which he and his enemy had their trouser legs nailed down side by side as they faced each other on a log over a swift stream. On that occasion the water had swept away Bowie's victim and his blood when Jim struck home with his knife, then slashed apart the clothing that bound them both to the log. He had outwitted Indian marauders, berserk runaway slaves, Mexican troops, and Gulf Coast pirates. It was no wonder people stared at him wherever he went, saying he had never lost a fight, just as he had never started one.

The other side of Jim Bowie most people did not know. This was his continual restlessness in the pursuit of

money. Born in Logan County, Kentucky, in 1796, Jim
Bowie had a gift for making money such as few men ever
know—and an equal one for letting it slip through his
hands. In this, it was said, he seldom let the law stand
in his way. He had, after all, as a daredevil youngster in
Rapides Parish, Louisiana, overcome natural laws, breaking
in wild mustangs and riding on the backs of alligators—
learning in the latter feat how to grab the upper jaw and
gouge the eyes, so that the alligator would stay afloat but
could not see what he was doing. He and his brothers had
only to learn how to outwit the milder laws of government.
By the age of eighteen he was already buying land near the
family farm and sawing and shipping timber downstream
to the New Orleans market. But this was tame compared to
the money that could be made from slaves. One had only
to know the right people—say pirate Jean Lafitte, who had
moved his smuggling operations from the Louisiana seashore
to Texas' Galveston Island. . . .

Within two years Jim and his older brothers, John
and Rezin, had made $65,000 smuggling slaves with the help
of Jean Lafitte. The remarkable thing was that they managed—almost—to stay within the law. The plan was an
ingenious one and drew nothing but praise from Jean
Lafitte, who admired the daring of the youngest Bowie
brother, claiming he always noted his resemblance to himself. The Bowies would pay Lafitte one dollar per pound
for a slave. While it was illegal to bring slaves in, it was
not, once they were smuggled into the country, illegal to
sell them. When the sheriff apprehended smuggled slaves,
he sold them at public auction. The Bowies made of this
a surefire system. They reported the presence of slaves—
their own—to the sheriff, then bought them at a dollar

per pound, winning a fifty-cent rebate on each pound as premium for having furnished the authorities with information. Now legal owners of slaves that had cost them $1.50 per pound, they could sell them at the current market price of about $1,000 per slave. The average slave weighed 140 pounds.

It was this sort of Bowie ingenuity that shortly carried the eldest brother, John, to the Arkansas state legislature, where he served three terms. Rezin and Jim, after running up a profit of $90,000 from their Louisiana steam mill—the first in the state for grinding sugar cane—were not far behind. When next heard from, the Bowie brothers, led by John, were selling land in Arkansas, secured, allegedly, from one Bernard Sampeyreac, who was said to have got the titles in 1789 from the Spanish governor Miró. In all, more than a hundred deeds had been sold to Arkansas business men when the Supreme Court pronounced Sampeyreac as fictitious as his unlikely name, and declared the land titles forged and fraudulent. The Bowies suffered no ostracism; John retained his post in his state legislature, and Rezin secured one soon after. They were only doing what many another man had been doing in territory that had been claimed first by France, then Spain, and now the United States. Meanwhile Jim Bowie, land-hungry and money-hungry, had come to Texas. And he had found the girl he wanted to marry.

It was Stephen F. Austin who put Bowie in touch with the Veramendi family of San Antonio de Béxar after his first attempts to locate silver mines had failed. Vice-governor Juan Veramendi was Texas' leading Mexican citizen, a brilliant man as fond of big-money schemes as Jim Bowie. Veramendi also had a beautiful young daughter who was kin to most of the ruling Mexican clans in Texas and Coahuila. Shortly Bowie became a Roman Catholic in a public ceremony in Béxar, though there is evidence he had been a Catholic during his youth in Louisiana. And shortly he became a Mexican citizen.

It was during the trip which was the occasion of his Mexican citizenship that he first acquired the right to buy fantastically large amounts of Texas land. Texas colonists were limited by law to a league each—4.428.4 acres. In 1830, however, Jim Bowie accompanied the Veramendi family to Saltillo, Mexican capital of the state of Coahuila and Texas. When he returned, he held—in addition to his citizenship from the Legislature—options to title for almost a million acres of Texas land. Since as a Mexican citizen he was entitled to buy only eleven leagues, or 50,000 acres, it was obvious his powerful friend had been at work, persuading Mexicans he knew in Saltillo to apply for their grants and sell or turn title over to Bowie. It was no wonder that the Mexican vice-governor of San Antonio de Béxar, sensing in Bowie the same land-hunger he himself felt, began thinking of Bowie as a prospective partner and son-in-law.

On April 23, 1831, after the customarily long Mexican courtship, Jim Bowie and Ursula de Veramendi were married. It was a successful marriage from many points of view. Despite the fact that Bowie remained restless and was on the move constantly, staying home only long enough to beget, it was clear that he had made a brilliant marriage. Ursula's father accepted Bowie as son and kept the couple supplied with money, giving them almost $2,000 for their wedding trip to New Orleans and Natchez, where Jim Bowie proudly showed off his bride to his family and his friends. She was a success everywhere, as lovely in her character as in her person. For the trip, Bowie also borrowed $750 from Ursula's grandmother, giving a note in security. They might have toured the world with the sum Jim had.

Curiously, Veramendi was in turn cautious about his son-in-law's finances. Bowie, after all, was a foreigner and nationally notorious. Veramendi caused him, therefore, to sign an amazing marriage contract. In it Bowie was the one to bring the dowry, pledging himself to settle $15,000 on his wife. Bowie listed his assets, totaling—on paper—almost a quarter of a million dollars. He neglected to say that $98,000 of his assets were notes of Arkansas purchasers of fraudulent and forged land titles. Bowie misrepresented his age, giving it as thirty instead of thirty-five.

Despite all this, the marriage was off to a brilliant start. The daughter of an innkeeper at Gonzales, seeing the Bowies on their honeymoon, recorded her admiration for the beautiful Ursula, though she could not but regret that the magnetic Jim Bowie was out of circulation—this despite the fact that Bowie had never pursued women, having, as his friend Cephas Ham had it, "an excessive reverence" for them. And seven months later, when they were presented at a party given for them on Christmas Day, Capt. William G. Hunt, impressed by their happiness, noted that Mrs. Bowie was a "beautiful Castilian lady," who won all hearts by her sweet manners. "Bowie was supremely happy with her," he wrote later, "very devoted and more like a kind and tender lover than the terrible duellist he had *since* been represented to be." The qualifying phrase probably reflected the growing criticism of Bowie and his Mexican ways by the War Party.

After a short stay at a villa of Ursula's father's near the San Jose mission, they returned to the Veramendi palace, living in a wing of the pleasant house whose garden sloped down to the tree-lined river banks. But marriage could not resolve Bowie's restlessness for long. Soon he was back on horseback, looking for land, for lost mines, for more land. Only the appearance, according to Mexican custom, of a new child each year testified to the happiness of his marriage.

Bowie was living as he had always lived—by his wits —still conducting his business on horseback; but now, with the influence of his father-in-law behind him, more ambitious projects appeared. His experience in the sugar industry, in slave trading, and in his land speculations had convinced Bowie that trade was the quickest source of profit —far more than the lost gold mines the Indians were forever telling him about. He and Veramendi, therefore, now launched a cotton textile mill in far-off Saltillo. Other business ventures took them to the rival city of Monclova, where the Veramendi family had a summer home in the healthful cool of the mountains. It was a good partnership—that between the land-hungry promoter and his equally ambitious banker—and had not tragedy struck in 1833 Bowie and his father-in-law might have altered the map of America—and of Mexico.

In 1826, cholera had broken out in Lower Bengal. In 1829, it was in Teheran, near the Caspian Sea. In the autumn of 1831, the plague hit Hamburg, moving ironically always over the same trade routes that brought men like Veramendi and Bowie money and fame. In 1832 a ship bringing immigrants to America from Dublin arrived at the

St. Lawrence. Forty-two of its passenger list of 145 were dead.

Jim Bowie did not expect to be touched by this epidemic that had already reached St. Louis. When word came that it was in New Orleans, brought down the Mississippi by boat, he did not defer his visit there. He was on an important land deal. At least his family would be safe. Ursula, at Jim's urging, had gone to Monclova with their two children and her mother and father. They could not be safer than in the mountain air of that resort, where he expected to join them after he finished his work in perhaps September or October.

He was in the plague-stricken area of Natchez when he heard the news, and it was neither October nor September that he returned to Monclova. When he came it was to pray at his family's graves. Within three days' time, from the fifth to the eighth of September, Bowie's wife, his two children, Mrs. Bowie's father and mother and other members of the family, all were struck down by the cholera.

Ursula Bowie's uncle, J. M. Navarro, wrote to one of Stephen Austin's lieutenants, Samuel M. Williams, asking him to break the news to Bowie. Navarro wrote: "When I told you my fears of the cholera it looks as if I had a sad premonition, because my brother-in-law, Veramendi, my sister Josefa, his wife, and Ursula Bowie and her children, died unexpectedly in Monclova . . . Madero died also. Three days illness were enough—from the 5th to the 8th of this month—to end all these precious lives. In fact during the first 18 days of this month 571 persons died. . . ."

Bowie was shaken as he had never been before. Noah

Smithwick, seeing him just after he learned the news, recorded that "strong man that he was," tears had coursed "down his cheeks while lamenting her untimely death. . . ."

After doing what was necessary in Monclova, he rushed back to his mother's place in Louisiana as though he never wanted to see Texas again. He had made out his will on the last day of October, 1833. Having already lived a life that would have killed an ordinary man, perhaps he wanted only to remain in seclusion among his own family until the day he died.

But he had lived too long in the dry, electric air of Béxar, and the spell of Texas was upon him. By Christmas he was back in the province again, a lost man. But this time he was not searching for the fabled San Saba gold mine. He was searching for the meaning of his existence.

JIM BOWIE sometimes asked himself how he had got to the Alamo, how of all the places he might have been he had come to be co-commander of an old mission with the one man on earth—William B. Travis—who could never understand him. Some of his feelings about his own destiny had emerged in a speech he had made to the delegates of the Texas Consultation of 1835. His lot had been cast, he had told his audience, "in a day and among a people rendered necessarily, from political and material causes, more or less independent of law." In exchange, he pointed out, the people of the frontier were "generous and scornful of every species of meanness and duplicity."

Bowie had been drinking more than a little, and went on to pour his scorn on the "double-dealing, unspeakable cowards" who were trying to besmirch his reputation. He explained that yielding to the dictates of his own heart, he had taken to his bosom as a wife "a true and lovely woman of a different country, the daughter of a distinguished Coahuil-Texano;" yet, as a thief in the night, death had invaded his home and taken his wife, his little ones, and his father-in-law. Now, standing alone of all his blood in Texas, all he asked was the privilege of serving it in the field.

Lieutenant-Governor James Robinson had said the council was astonished, not knowing that Jim Bowie was such a natural orator....

His feelings had been genuine, however, for when he returned from his Louisiana homeplace, he came as a different man. His grief was still great within him, and according to those who knew him he now did two things on a gigantic scale: he drank steadily and he schemed for ever-larger holdings in Texas land.

Jim Bowie had not had to worry about money while he was a Veramendi son-in-law. One of Ursula's kin testified in court, at one of the estate suits, that "Mrs. Bowie's father made no further provision for her than that she and Colonel Bowie lived in the midst of the Veramendi family.... Colonel Bowie had no visible property but Mrs. Bowie's father furnished her and her husband with money and supplies without limit up to the time of her death."

Now, with his father-in-law dead of cholera, Bowie had once more to think of ways and means. Surprisingly, friends seemed always ready to subsidize him, in amounts ranging anywhere from $4,000 to $20,000. Angus McNeil, whom Bowie had commissioned to buy in Boston $20,000 worth of machinery for the textile mill Bowie and Veramendi had been planning, reported that Bowie "was a splendid man of the most fascinating manners, exceedingly lavish in the expenditure of money" with "an extraordinary capacity for getting money from his friends." Yet what he gained—from friends or land—always disappeared in a hurry. His talent for losing money—probably in gambling and drink—was as great as his talent for pursuing it.

In 1833, at the time he heard of Ursula's death, Bowie had lain very sick, tended by Dr. Richardson, at Angus McNeil's home in Natchez. Two years later, these two witnesses of his suffering that day came to Texas with him on a grandiose land project. McNeil and Dr. Richardson reached Nacogdoches with Bowie in the autumn of 1835. Dr. Richardson had $80,000 in his pocket, which had been entrusted to him by a company to invest in land. Dr. Richardson, McNeil said, had twice "attended Bowie in dangerous attacks of sickness and was very much under his influence, as were most of his other friends." Bowie could easily have obtained from the generous doctor, McNeil said, any reasonable amount of money.

He did. But Bowie also persuaded the doctor to stay in Texas—to stay despite the threat of an invasion from Santa Anna. There was only one way to meet that kind of threat—join the Texas army and fight it off. They had, after all, only to drive out Santa Anna to make that $80,000 pay off handsomely. Not to mention the property of 6,500,000 acres of Texas land granted the New York company of land shark John T. Mason, whose deputy administrator was James Bowie. . . .

The number of acres was the important thing. First a million—then six million—there was no stopping in this gigantic land. The land, after all, could become a wife to a man—yes, a wife, and a child too. . . .

IT WAS Jim Bowie's extensive holdings of Texas land that caused him to disobey Sam Houston's order to blow up the Alamo—that and his essential independence.

Bowie was accustomed to making his own laws, and like every other Texas leader—Fannin, Houston, Johnson, Travis—he hoped sooner or later to be recognized as the real military expert of the region. He had proved his prowess as a Texas Ranger in subduing the Indians, as a volunteer commander in defeating Mexican Colonel Piedras in a minor fray at Nacogdoches in 1832, by his impressive feats at Mission Concepcíon and in the Grass Fight, both in the autumn of 1835. His national reputation proclaimed him the champion of knife fighters.

Bowie interpreted Sam Houston's order of January 17, 1836, to destroy the mission fort, therefore, as only another test of his independent judgment. Who, after all, knew Texas better than he did? With Colonel Neill's approval—and later Travis's—he decided San Antonio was the "key to Texas" that must never be abandoned.

But Travis and the others were motivated by a dream —the dream of establishing a magnificent Aaron Burr type of Republic of the Southwest. It was for this that they planned to march straight to the "halls of Montezuma" to incorporate the wealth of Mexico's silver and gold into the Texas Commonwealth. Bowie meanwhile was thinking only of defending the land—his land—his million Texas acres.

It was one of the few decisions upon which Travis and Bowie agreed. From the arrival of Travis on February 3, almost a month behind Bowie, to the first day of the siege, the conflict between the two men had been continuous and undisguised. It started because of a question of rank.

Bowie had appealed to the convention in November for a high command to allow him to recruit a large number of troops, a certainty in view of his great personal popularity. He harangued the council and left. No action was taken at the time. If he had any official rank, no one knew of it, but the men called him colonel from his title in the Texas Rangers.

When Colonel Neill had to leave the Alamo in mid-February, he had a problem. Travis was a colonel—in fact he regarded himself as commander in chief—of the Texas cavalry. Neill liked Bowie and wanted to leave him in command, but his duty was to pass on the assignment to the regular army man, Travis. Knowing this would displease the men left at the Alamo, of whom three-quarters were volunteers like Bowie himself, Neill named Travis and tried to slip away before the news got out. He failed. The men caught him as he was about to leave, brought him back and sat him down till he agreed they could elect their own leader.

These volunteers elected Bowie. Travis chose to assume this was supplementary to his own command of the regular army, even though there was indeed a minority present. He assumed Bowie was to command only the volunteer troops. Bowie on the other hand, smarting from neglect by Stephen F. Austin and by the council, and having no desire to turn over command to a youth still in his twenties, a youth who seemed to despise all the things Bowie valued, chose to regard his as total command. He and Travis had never liked each other. Now the battle began.

The letter of J. J. Baugh, adjutant of the Post of Béxar, to Governor Smith on February 13 consisted largely of a summary of the succeeding skirmishes. Stating that Travis could not submit to the control of Bowie, while Bowie, availing himself of his popularity, was eager for total command, Baugh continued:

Things passed on in this way yesterday and today until at length they have become intolerable. Bowie as commander of the volunteers, has gone so far as to stop carts laden with goods of private families removing into the country. He has ordered the Prison doors to be opened for the release of a Mexican convicted of theft who had been tried by a jury of 12 men among which was Col. Travis and Col. Bowie himself.

He has also ordered and effected the release of D. H. Barre, a private in the Regular Army attached to the Legion of Cavalry, who had been tried by a Court Martial and found guilty of desertion and actually deliberated him from Prison with a Corporal's Guard with loud huzzas: But the most extraordinary step of all and that which sets aside all law, Civil and Military is that which follows

Commandancy of Bejar
Feb. 13th 1836

Capt of Corps—
You are hereby required to release such Prisoners as may be under your direction for labor or otherwise
James Bowie
Commander of Volunteer forces of Bejar....

Antonio Fuentes who had been released ... presented himself to the judge ... and demanded his clothes which were in the Calaboose, stating that Col Bowie had set him at Liberty, whereupon the judge (Seguin) ordered him remanded to prison.... As soon as this fact was reported to Bowie, he went in a furious manner, and demanded of the judge a release of the prisoner, which the Judge refused saying that "he would give up his office and let the Military appoint a judge." Bowie immediately sent to the Alamo for troops and paraded in the Square under Arms in a tumultuously and disorderly manner. Bowie, himself and many of his men being drunk which has been the case ever since he has been in command. . . .

The effect of this freeing of any Mexicans who could help scout, forage, or spy was to infuriate the young Travis as it delighted the older Bowie. It is no wonder that the twenty-seven-year-old co-commander wrote his governor, two days after Bowie's election: "My situation is truly awkward and delicate. . . ."

What shocked him primarily was Bowie's drunkenness. Bowie, he wrote, "was elected by two small companies and since his election has been roaring drunk all the time."

The stages of drunkenness on the frontier were relative. Whisky was the standard frontier remedy against sickness—and everybody knew Bowie since the loss of his wife was a man sick unto death, now living on his nerves. There is a difference, however, between companionable gaiety and besottedness, as Travis well knew. What really vexed him appeared in his next charge: "[Bowie] has assumed all command and is proceeding in a most disorderly and irregular manner—interfering with private property, releasing prisoners sentenced by court martial & by the civil court & turning everything topsy turvy."

There is as much revelation about Travis as about Bowie in the letter. Travis continued: "If I didn't feel my honor and that of my country comprometted, I would leave here instantly for some other point with the troops under my immediate command as I am unwilling to be responsible for the drunken irregularities of any man." The irritation of remaining here when there was glory to be found elsewhere was now being directed toward Bowie.

In all of this Bowie knew what he was doing. He liberated specifically two Mexicans who might be of use to the Texans—one accused of desertion from the army and the other of theft. Since Bowie had been a minority dissenter on the jury for the latter, he was simply applying the verdict he had originally voted. The one accused of desertion was one of his own agents. Most of all, Bowie wanted to show Travis simultaneously a lesson in tolerance toward Mexicans and to show him who was running the show. All Bowie now had left was his pride—and his ability, he would have called it his manhood, for holding liquor. The entire quarrel had been no more than a middle-aged man's need to prove himself again at the threat of youthful competition. Unknowingly, of course, the twenty-seven-year-old Travis had humiliated him.

Travis must have understood this shortly, for the next day he and Bowie composed a joint letter to "His Excellency H. Smith, Governor of Texas" to say that "henceforth all general orders and correspondence will be signed by both." This was not mere coexistence of volunteer command and regular command; both men were recognizing the other's strengths. But they were not yet friends, and would never be. And the loyalty of the men went out, not to the regular army man, but to the ailing, hard-drinking Bowie.

This was the man, then, who on the morning of February 24, 1836, took a detail up a timber scaffolding

to work on a cannon that was being mounted. It was
Tuesday morning, and the second day of the siege. . . .

DURING THE last two months Bowie and the post's chief
engineer, Green B. Jameson, had placed most of the guns,
the four-pounders and the eights and twelves. If installation
was not complete it was because the volunteers comprising
three-fourths of the garrison had no appetite for work
when they were without pay. Green Jameson, like Bowie
and Travis, had composed letters to Governor Smith and
to Major General Sam Houston begging for money. But
money was what the Texas government did not have. It
had land aplenty to give volunteers, but it had no cash
and the appeals went unanswered. Jameson complained
that officers were having to do all the work, even patrol
duty. You could not get labor, or even daily drill, out of a
volunteer who had received only seven dollars in cash in
the past four months. One youth had complained he did
not even have the eighth part of a sectored silver dollar,
or "bit," to pay for getting his shirt washed. Even if he
kept on wearing it dirty, there were other needs the
volunteers felt. They were thirsty. Some of the men had
to pawn their rifles to get their requirements of whiskey
and *aguardiente*. Several came into the Alamo for the last
ditch fight without weapons.

But now that the Mexican army was here and sustain-
ing a steady fusillade, the Texans worked hard to finish
duties they had halfheartedly begun. The Alamo garrison
had enough food to last a month; their powder was poor
and scant, but would last a fortnight if sparingly used. They
needed firewood (a peach orchard several hundred yards

away looked likely), they needed men, they needed ammunition, they needed points of defense—all the things that the Alamo, built for a mission and not a fortress, could not provide.

What they did have, until reinforcements arrived from Goliad and the thousands of volunteers from the States poured over the border, was artillery. Not in great amount, but perhaps enough to keep Santa Anna's 6,000 men at bay for a few days. Sharpshooting would not do it, nor would hand-to-hand fighting if the enemy ever got that close.

Luckily, already a score of cannon were mounted or ready to be placed. The one Bowie was placing now was on a fifteen-foot platform, shored up with a mound of earth, in the southern half of the fort's main plaza. It was the only free-standing cannon emplacement the Texans made, the only one not against a wall.

It was another clear day, the sun giving respite from the wet weather that had marred much of the winter in normally mild San Antonio, and Bowie, standing on the above-wall-height scaffold, surveying the hoisting of the twelve-pounder by earthen ramps, pulleys, and cables, was grateful for it. His cough had been causing him trouble all winter—Dr. Sutherland had always told him he was the one man at the Alamo he couldn't cure—and it was good simply to stand in the warm sun and let it draw the sickness from his body. He was forty years old and sick with an illness he did not even want to name, though in his own solitude he admitted to himself it was tuberculosis and knew he would never get away from it, as long as he lived. . . .

Shouting an order, he grasped the wheel spokes

roughly and put his weight behind it. The Mexican batteries were going at it in earnest now. He wondered how long these 150 men could defend the three-acre area that required six times their number. He was thinking of them, and of their plight, when the accident occurred.

A seizure of violent coughing gripped him. Half-blind, he let go the spokes for a moment. The cannon pivoted and there were sudden shouts of alarm. Men below jumped back hastily. Bowie massed his weight and strained his sinews to stop the cannon from rolling off.

For minutes they remained that way—Bowie and the fiercest enemy he had ever struggled with in hand-to-hand combat. Then the cannon stopped rolling. Bowie had steadied it but at his own peril. Before the startled gaze of the men below, he plummeted straight to the earth, his ribs crushed into his chest.

He was only dimly conscious of the cries of the men who rushed to him or of their anxious questions as they got him on an improvised stretcher. He had suffered a terrible concussion. In the dimmest part of his consciousness he was aware that they were taking him to the hospital quarters at the south end of the main barracks. The Mexican batteries were pounding away, the balls occasionally hitting the barracks quarters. But Jim Bowie was not thinking of them or of the damage they did. In the fever of his brain he was thinking of death, his old enemy who had come in the night to steal his wife and children, and was now coming to steal his Texas land. . . .

6

There were some who said William Barret Travis had singlehandedly started the war against Mexico. That a war would have come sooner or later was a certainty, but there was no denying that Travis played an important role in it.

It had started when he arrived in Texas, leaving his wife and two-year-old son in Claiborne, Alabama, after having carefully and dutifully consigned to her all his savings and property. It was a characteristic gesture of the six-foot-tall, auburn-haired youth who seemed at times to exist for a sense of duty. The Travises were staunch Baptists—Travis's own uncle had founded the Baptist stronghold of Evergreen College in Alabama—and the young lawyer had grown up expecting as much of himself as his rigorous code caused him to expect of others.

It was this code which inflamed him into action upon his arrival in Texas. Outraged at the injustice of Mexican demands upon the settlers, he had been particularly infuriated by the establishing of a new customs collector at Anáhuac, near Galveston. This collector was actually a renegade Kentuckian, John Davis Bradburn, more despotic than the despot he now served. Twice at the customs post Travis had constituted himself a one-man army to vanquish Mexican pettiness and tyranny. The first time, in 1832, he had been imprisoned for fifty days by Bradburn. The second attempt had succeeded. If he was at the Alamo now confronting Santa Anna, it was largely because in June, 1835, gathering his friends together, he had chased out Santa Anna's deputy, Captain Antonio Tenorio, from his post. It was a bold move and the Texas settlers condemned him for "precipitating war." But when Santa Anna demanded that Travis be turned over to the Mexican government for punishment, the colonists rose in his defense. Even the patient Stephen F. Austin had finally agreed that the only Texan answer to military occupation was recourse to war.

If Travis was a good man to start a war, the hotheaded youth was an equally good one to fight it. This became increasingly clear to the men as news of Bowie's accident now spread. The initial hopes that he might recover faded as the truth became known. Bowie, who had already burned up the equivalent of several lifetimes in his four decades of wanderlust and whose tuberculosis was generally known, was now delirious with fever and typhoid-pneumonia. The new commander was Travis, and Travis only.

It was not, at first, an easy transition for the men

to make. It seemed a long way from the companion in drink who had led them ten days before in the parade in the Square to the youth whose gray-blue eyes always fixed one with such intensity. Bowie had stood for everything lawless, and it still thrilled the men to recall that wild parade of arms, that snake dance, that hootenanny of a revolt against pompous respectability that said they were men of a special stripe.

But Travis was a man of a special stripe, too. He had shown that in yesterday's oath of no surrender, a gesture worthy of Bowie. He showed it now, simply in the way his eyes glowed, the way he spoke as if there was no doubt who was in command. It was true he stood for duty; it was true he was a puritan of a special sort. But perhaps William Barret Travis would not have been the Roman soldier he was—and one among them had to be—if he had not been streaked with that layer of puritanism. And it was a streak, and not the whole man.

THE MEN who doubted that Travis was quite human would have felt quite differently if they had seen his diary. The men of the time were given to reviewing their lives, and Travis, like many another, had kept not only a diary but also what he called a commonplace book in which he could write down his thoughts. The figure that emerges from the pages of the diary he kept from 1833 to 1834 at San Felipe was far from the remote, chronically unhappy puritan some of his associates thought him to be. The man who could write, on March 21, 1834, "Horse loose—could not be caught—spent day pleasantly—*in la sociedad de mi inamorata*" and on June 22: "Went to

Clay's—Bot whiskey for Kendy—paid 3 cts—Whitesides', Coles—Adventure with Miss T—&c—" was no silently suffering saint.

But suffer he did, and while his diary tells little of his feelings concerning his marriage and separation, it reveals enough to show that mingled with the happy youth full of gusto at seeing the new land of Texas in 1831 was the man who never quite recovered from the memory of Rosanna Travis, whom he had left, expecting a second child, in Claiborne, Alabama.

It was something he never mentioned upon his arrival in Texas when, in 1831, he was seeking land grants in both Stephen F. Austin's colony and in that of Ben Milam. Even in the oath which he took as a colonist, he described himself in one case as a widower and in the other as a bachelor. Rosanna E. Travis and her second child—Susan Isabelle—were not mentioned.

Nor did he discuss the event which had brought him to Texas. Whether he had killed the Claiborne citizen in a fit of anger for casting aspersions on Mrs. Travis, or because he had been intimate with her, or whether it was not Travis but a friend of the family who had murdered the insulter, Travis never said. It was known only that the man had died.

Travis's reaction to Texas was one of instantaneous approval. While it is true he wrote a letter to the *Christian Advocate* inviting Methodist missionaries to vitalize the dormant religious life of Texas, he obviously loved the daily round of existence he led in Stephen F. Austin's namesake town, San Felipe de Austin, recording in his diary, without much sense of selection or emphasis, every detail of what happened each day. The diary opens, in fact, with his enthusiastic response on August 31, 1833, to his new home, this "pretty country" of Austin's settlement.

He was practicing law in San Felipe, doing remarkably well, and making many friends: Travis had at all times a remarkable gift for friendship and was always quick to help with money or attention when a friend fell ill. He was even, at twenty-four, developing literary aspirations, and was reading widely—Sir Walter Scott; straight history, from Herodotus to memoirs of Napoleon, and, reassuringly, even of Josephine; and sophisticated books like *Roderick Random*, which he read in two days.

In many ways the picture was one of complete success. The number of clients he had won as lawyer and the fees he recorded show that he was a talented advocate, one well aware of his own worth. Among his friends— with whom he often talked and drank well into the night —were Moseley Baker, his neighbors the Townsends, and a leader of the Texas War Party, Judge R. M. Williamson —among the most influential people in San Felipe. Judge Williamson, known as "Three-Legged Willie" because of the stump leg he wore, was an especially close friend. A self-styled poet, he contributed verse to the San Felipe newspaper, and reprinted his favorite poet, Byron, in the *Gazette* until Byron became the most widely read poet in Texas. When Williamson ran for office, Travis electioneered for him and placed bets on his victory, which paid off. The two lawyers started sending each other clients, and Travis prospered so rapidly, he engaged young John Kuykendall as his assistant.

But his separation from Rosanna Travis, with whom he remained in correspondence, was hurting both of them. The letters seemed more and more distant as months changed into years. Finally they began coming from her brother. In the meantime Travis had met a girl named Rebecca Cummins (as he spelled it in his diary) or Cummings.

There is ample evidence in the diary that Travis was healthily and abundantly interested in women. Entries like "Went to Mill Creek on Huff's horse—Hell—L-v-e triumphed over slander &c—staid all night at C's" and "Staid all night at Chriesman—pretty country—Miss J—" make it very clear that his puritanism was no match for his desires. Rebecca Cummins was different, however. She lived with her family at nearby Mill Creek, and they had met, it was said, one day when he had been lost near the Cummins farm. By the time Governor Smith was to order him to the Alamo, Rosanna and he were divorced, and he and Rebecca Cummins had become engaged.

The entries in the diary concerning Travis's wife are cryptic and, like the others, written in a telegraphic style. On September 3, 1833, he noted: "Recd letter from R. E. Travis—*malo*—wrote to R. E. Travis—& Wm. M. Cato—Senor Flores—an European Spaniard." Rosanna Travis has become the neuter "R.E." Her brother was writing him too, and on November 1, two months later, he recorded he "endorsed $10 bill to R. E. Travis." Far more significant was the note on January 9, 1834: "Recd letter from Wm. M. Cato—answered same—Recd letter from R. E. Travis —answered same. She is willing to give up my son Charles to me. I directed him to be sent to Brazoria to the care of Mrs. Long." On the next day he sent Monroe Edwards to Alabama to bring his son to Texas. On that day he wrote again to Rosanna and to William M. Cato, as he did to the latter on the following day once more, and to

Rosanna again on the day after that. It was clear he wanted no hitch in the plan to get his son away from his wife—and equally clear that his strong paternal feeling was breaking through. He had a great fondness for children, giving them money, buying candy for them, even trying once to find Sunday School literature for them, only to discover he could not find a Bible to buy in San Felipe.

If he loved the child more, it now became clear he loved the wife less. He wanted nothing from Rosanna but the recovery of his son—and a divorce. On Sunday, March 20, one of the many Sundays he spent with the Cummins family, he wrote: "Sunday—pleasant—Arrangement to wait till divorce is effected—& then—*a casar con* ———" The long blank was a discreet substitute for Rebecca Cummins, who had now replaced Rosanna Travis in his affections. The use of Spanish for "and then to get married to ———" was not for privacy but for emotional release. Like many another man, he had discovered that "Spanish is a loving tongue" and learned that he could shake off inhibitions better in a foreign language.

The courtship, and the weekly Sunday visits that furthered it, was not without its annoyances. For every entry that read "Staid all night at Cummins—Gave R. a breast pin—& took lock of hair &c—" or "Went to Mill Creek—swam twice—good ducking—narrow escape—*Tengo buena Fortuna en el amor de la senorita—Mostró una carta a ella sobre el conducto de la mujer de antes—*&c. [I am lucky in the love of the young lady—I showed her a letter on the conduct of her predecessor]" there were many that read "Went to Cummins'—*recepción frio, pero conclusion muy caliente* [a cold reception, but a very warm conclusion]." Rebecca had her reasons for turning hot and cold, primarily her need for assurance that she had really replaced Rosanna in Travis's affections.

She had other rivals than Rosanna to worry about, however. On Christmas Eve Travis recorded: "Reading Herodotus &c—*Mandaba la carta que yo escribí ayer, a la senorita de H—— por la negrita Ruda y pagaba a ella un peso—$1. Tengo dos competidores para la mano de Ella—pagaba a Urban un peso que devo para Gloves— Pagaba la Malinda para lavando un peso—$1.00 &c.* [Sent the letter which I wrote yesterday to the Señorita de H—— by the Negress Ruda and paid her one peso. I have two competitors for Miss H's hand—paid Urban one peso I owed for gloves—paid Malinda one peso for washing.] Sent ball tickets, &c." And on Christmas Day: "Bought of Urban 2 bottles of cologne water $1.00—of Fletcher 1 oz. cinnamon—12½ *y mandaba ellos a la Senorita de H* [and had them sent to the Señorita de H]." The next day he went to a party at Major Lewis's, noted that La Senorita de H. was there and added cryptically, "A development &c." On December 29: "Paid for last night's fiddler 43¾ cts.—gave him 2 drinks charged at Cornell's"—and this final baffling note: "Hell among the women about party."

Occasionally, too, when he was not reading such books as *Vivien Grey, Court and Camp of Bonaparte*, and the play *Westward Ho*—borrowed from his neighbors, the Townsends—he took time for gambling. On January 16, he wrote, he went on a "gambling spree," and was still playing the cards with bad luck as late as February 1, when he lost $36 at faro and $30 at bravo. His losses that year surpassed his winnings by $200.

He was never away from Rebecca Cummins for long, however, and the 1833–1834 diary closed with the entry of

June 25th: "Staid all night at Cummins's—reconciliation—happy &c—" The use of the ampersand was one he never discarded.

For all the brevity of the entries, no one could deny that the Travis who wrote in his diary was a greatly different man from the commander the men knew—or thought they knew—at the Alamo.

He was a man who had swum rivers at night to be with his beloved. He was a man of many friends and great generosity, a soft touch for a loan. Rather than eating his heart out for his young wife and son, he was enjoying the company of Williamson, Townsend, Baker, and of Rebecca Cummins and the Senorita de la H.—and learning that Rosanna Cato was a woman of greater resources than might first appear.

But the pride, the immense pride the men at the Alamo sensed in him and that seemed to compensate in some way for the blow to his self-esteem inflicted by his flight from Alabama, was unmistakable. He was also, as the diary reveals, a bit vainglorious, worrying, even on the prairie, about his appearance. When he won a profitable case, he immediately ordered fancy new clothes, spending large sums on dress. He coddled his health and set down every penny he spent on it. And he was enormously pleased with himself and his new life, for he wrote his boyhood friend, Jim Bonham, to come on to Texas because "it is the land of the future."

Travis was not patient, like Stephen F. Austin; his was not a cool brain, like Jim Bowie's; he was not full of cunning, like Sam Houston; certainly not a hero like Davy Crockett. Of them all, he was the only one who had not spent his youth before coming to Texas. But he had enormous intensity. If he was bursting with energy and pride, it was the energy, pride, ambitiousness, and competitiveness of youth.

WILLIAM BARRET TRAVIS was to see his wife once more before going to the Alamo. In 1835, in the early autumn, Rosanna E. Travis made unaccompanied—except for her six-year-old son and her four-year-old daughter—the long trip to Texas to seek an understanding with her estranged husband, and make an arrangement about her son, Charles Edward Travis, now six years old. Travis, long eager to get the boy, had sent Monroe Edwards for him, but Rosanna chose to bring him herself, in the hopes of achieving a reconciliation.

By now her hopes were very slim. A year before, in requesting Judge Dellett to start proceedings for a divorce, she wrote:

> My friends advised me long since to seak a divorse, but as I had not lost confidence in his integrity to me, however deficient he may have been to others, I confided in his assurances to me, that he would return to his family or send for them as soon as he could obtain the means to make them comfortable, he continued to write to me affectionately and to repeat his assurances of unchanging attachment until my brother Wm took exception to his conduct toward me believing as he did that his intention was to abandon me all together and yet inspire me with the hope that he would return to or send for me until he could can [sic] no longer conceal his real designs of abandoning me alltogether."

She added that her brother wrote Travis "in plain language" his "suspitions of him." Travis had answered, she says, that he never planned to return and wished to be separated.

> After the declarations of such a wish on his part [she continued] I could no longer oppose my friends no matter how painful the thought may be ... Sir I must submit to this mortification with nothing but the knowledge of my own innocence....

Rosanna Travis closed the letter by saying:

> If anything occurred to dissatisfy him with me it was the result of my ignorance as to what was my duty as a wife, or I would have performed it to his entire satisfaction.

Now, in 1835, she was to try again, bringing both her children (in the opinion of Mrs. Holley, the cousin of Stephen F. Austin) in the hope that she might get him to resume normal family life. What she had not counted on, however, in the room in the small inn where the meeting took place, was the complete absence of love in William B. Travis after four years of separation. And she had not counted on seeing him in the company of Rebecca Cummins.

All hope died when she saw them together. It remained for her only to secure from him a statement that would enable her to get a divorce. Then she left, taking with her her daughter. The boy, Charles Edward, remained with Travis in Texas.

What William B. Travis did not know, as he sat at the scarred table in the headquarters room at the Alamo reviewing the events of his life, was that only two weeks before the beginning of Santa Anna's attack, Rosanna Cato was married to a wealthy Southern planter....

But Travis's mind was far from affairs of the heart. He was thinking of the increased noise from the Mexican shells outside and wondering how he could rouse the nation, now that he was in command—he alone, without Jim Bowie.

7

As dusk descended over the Mexican camp on February 24, the second day of the siege, and the guns continued their steady barrage, General Antonio Lopez de Santa Anna found, to his surprise, that he was not thinking about guns at all. All day he had hardly given a thought to these stupid *norteamericanos* and their mission fort. Instead he was thinking about women and the bride he had—to his delight and astonishment—married only a few hours before.

He had never expected such luck here in San Antonio, the town that had always plagued him with misfortune before. To be sure, he deserved it after the bitter and terrible two-month march. But so beautiful a girl—and after so short a time—it was beyond his wildest dream, enough to make him believe the gods had truly smiled on him when he was born.

Curiously enough, he had found the San Antonio beauty in the strict path of military duty. And, fortunately for him, the encounter coincided with his strategy of delay in attacking the Alamo.

He had known from the beginning that he could take the Texans by surprise attack if he so desired. They were so naive, he thought, so unwilling to face reality, disregarding, as he had heard, what every Mexican in San Antonio knew—that he had crossed the Rio Grande on February 16 with a force they could not possibly withstand. The weather had been against a surprise attack, however—the weather and the bell ringing that frightened off General Ramirez and his advance cavalry unit. Denied his pleasure by this and by the floods on the river, he would have to try an assault on the Alamo walls—or bide his time.

Though filled with contempt for the Texans, Santa Anna knew he would risk a terrific loss of personnel in a straight assault. The position of the Alamo fortress was too commanding, its walls strong enough to resist demolition by his light guns; he lacked heavy siege artillery. His only course was to bide his time. In a matter of hours he could surround the Alamo, prevent reinforcements from getting in. Then would come the pleasure of starving the garrison out. Still, it disturbed him not to destroy the upstart Anglos with one swift arrogant gesture. Santa Anna had the habit of contempt.

In the meantime there was the problem of crossing the San Antonio River, still swollen from the heavy winter rains and the cloudburst on the night of February 20. To close in his siege Santa Anna would have to bridge it at several points. Only one gangplank now led across it, at the foot of the main street.

Needing timber for these crossings, Santa Anna ordered the wrecking of several houses on the river banks. It was in one of these, on the slope down from the Alamo where the river made a horseshoe loop east, that General Castrillon had found the girl and her mother, living in shabby respectability. So enthusiastic was his description of the velvet-skinned beauty that Santa Anna had gone at once to see for himself, and had found his aide's taste excellent. He ordered the aide to secure the timber for the bridge—and the beauty for himself. Castrillon, Spanish-born and bred, executed the first request but demurred about the second. He did not regard the commandeering of young ladies for the general as a military order. As a general in the Mexican army, he had his self-respect.

If Castrillon would not be procurer for *El Presidente*, Colonel Miñon would. What better way could there be to please the general? In this case, however, he ran into the obstacle of the girl's mother.

The mother was adamant in her position. Her daughter was not only eminently respectable but also entitled to consideration. Her father, now dead, had once been an officer in the Mexican army. No proposition not honorable could be entertained for a moment, not even from so powerful and impetuous a lover as Santa Anna himself. The mother admired the general, but she admired marriage even more.

Santa Anna was not to be put thus aside. He had fought many battles. He could fight this doting mama of his new liquid-eyed *inamorata*.

Colonel Miñon, most sympathetic, agreed. He suggested a fake marriage. *Bravissimo!* Obviously Colonel Miñon was a man with a future—one who knew how to combine novelty with custom. And Miñon had other ideas. One of his underlings was well educated, gifted in languages, and expert at mimicry. With suitable habiliments, this gifted mimic might successfully impersonate a priest. It was only a matter of minutes.

In the afternoon of the second day of the siege, therefore, General Santa Anna and the girl were married at the general's headquarters in a ritualistic but very counterfeit ceremony according to the rites of the Church. The ceremony was accompanied by the steady sounds of cannon fire; the drumming of soldiers' feet, mostly barefooted in the mud, in maneuvers; the bells from San Fernando Church, and the lowing of cattle presently to be slaughtered for the military.

No man, Santa Anna told himself as he stood now outside the room where his bride was making herself ready, had ever been more fortunate. He would tire of her, of course. Tomorrow he would be ready for fighting again and would have to send her off. He had already told Colonel Miñon, in fact, "I shall send her to Mexico and save her for my old age." And she would go off like all the others, riding in his carriage and thinking herself First Lady of the land, though his wife in Mexico City would have been surprised to hear the girl call herself that.

But tonight it was hard to think what tomorrow's mood would be. There would be time tomorrow, and the day after tomorrow, he told himself, as he went in to his new bride, to think of the Texans and their stupid war. And time then to think of all the other women waiting for him in Mexico . . . waiting for his and their old age. . . .

THE MEN AT THE ALAMO meanwhile were thinking about food. The smell of barbecued beef at the end of a day of fighting was all that was needed to bring them back to themselves, and they went about it—those not on picket duty—with the gravest of faces as they cut slices of steak from the side of beef and barbecued them over the open wood fire. It was one of the beeves that had been corralled in the Mexican streets the day before. There were kitchen rooms in the mission convent, but the missionaries had long ago taken their equipment with them. The simplest way to cook meat as good as this was to broil it over an open fire and eat it with bowie knife and fingers.

They were fortunate in their cooks; there were many excellent, food-loving cooks in the Alamo, as the mingled smells of beef and peppered beans and tortillas testified. Mrs. Dickinson and the Mexican women were there. Travis's servant, the Negro boy Joe, and Bowie's slave boy Sam, were experts. And of course every frontiersman knew how to fix what he liked. Eating was good these first days, even though they had no coffee.

Unlike the Mexican soldiers, many of whom had been conscripted by emptying the jails of northern Mexico and for whom soldiering was a worse sentence than hard labor, the Texans in the Alamo were basically pioneers who were there by choice. Whereas two thousand Mexicans had deserted along the way, many to die of thirst in the desert, not one of these men had turned back. They remained because they thought they had a right to be there.

Like most Americans at the time, they thought that Thomas Jefferson had really bought Texas from Napoleon in 1803 as part of the Louisiana Purchase. Certainly Napoleon had laid the grounds for this belief when he resurrected French claims to Texas, based on La Salle's small settlement on the Gulf Coast. In 1819, when the United States government, in a treaty with Spain, had taken Florida in exchange for giving up any claim to Texas, the howl of protest had been nationwide. Texas was so clearly a natural extension of the frontier of a nation headed straight across the continent to the Pacific; how could its borders ever be defined?

They were of all ages, the men in the Alamo, and of every conceivable type. The oldest man around the fire was Robert B. Moore, a Virginian who had come to Texas by way of New Orleans. He was a private. The gayest was Davy Crockett, cracking jokes. "Pelting us with apples," he observed scornfully of the Mexican cannon balls. One present was a Baptist minister, William Garnett. He was one of the youngest, only twenty-four, and was an outspoken admirer of Travis. He had settled at Robertson's Colony at the Falls of the Brazos and his friends testified that he was a man of unblemished character.

The three Taylor brothers—George, twenty-two; James, twenty; Edward, eighteen—were also at the fire, as was Tapley Holland, who was twenty-four and had been living in Texas since he was ten. The Taylor brothers came from the town of Liberty, Texas, near where La Salle was killed by his crazed followers. Tapley Holland also had two brothers in the Texan army. All three Hollands had fought together with Jim Bowie at Concepción; Tapley was now alone at the Alamo.

Dr. Amos Pollard, Massachusetts-born, New York-trained, also watched the flames. On October 23, 1835, Stephen F. Austin had appointed him "surgeon of the regiment," within a week of his thirty-second birthday. Pollard had just established his home in Gonzales, after leaving his wife and baby daughter in New Orleans while he joined a company of "adventurers bound for Texas."

Of all the men united here, few were more colorful than Micajah Autry. He was a gentleman; like Austin and a number of other Texas settlers, he had acquired a good education in the States. He was a scholar, a teacher, poet, painter, and lawyer. Though forty-three, he was a private and one of "Davy Crockett's boys." When Travis answered Santa Anna's blood-red flag on the first day with a blast from the Texans' eighteen-pounder, Micajah Autry was among the men who pounded in the powder, primed the cannon, and blew defiance at the dictator.

Micajah Autry fought as a youth in the War of 1812, and the experience ruined his health. Moving from his native North Carolina to Tennessee, he found farming too rigorous, and turned to the law, with immediate success. Soon he was able to get married. But he made the mistake, he said, of thinking he was gifted for the mercantile business. In 1835, he was in Louisiana and wrote back home that

the impulse to Texas, both as to soldiers and as to moving families, exceeds anything I have known. I have little doubt that the army will receive ample supplies from New Orleans both of provisions and munitions of war, as the people of Texas have formed themselves into something like a government. I have had many glowing descriptions of the country by those who have been there. . . . We have between 400 and 500 miles to foot it to the seat of the government, for we cannot get horses, but we have sworn allegiance to each other and will get along somehow.

The last letter he wrote his wife was from Nacogdoches.

> My dear Martha [he wrote] I have reached this point
> after many hardships and privations, but thank God in
> most excellent health. The very great fatigue I have suf
> fered has in a degree stifled reflection and has been an
> advantage to me. I walked from Natchitoches, whence I
> wrote you last, to this place 115 miles through a torrent
> of rain, mud and water. We expect to march to headquar
> ters [Washington-on-the-Brazos] 125 miles from here,
> where we shall join Houston, the commander-in-chief,
> and receive our destination. I may or may not receive pro
> motion, as there are many very meritorious men seeking
> the same.

Autry was proud of his companions. He called them
"a very select company of men, including four lawyers."
He assured his wife that he had become one of the most
thorough-going men she had ever heard of: "I go the
whole Hog in the cause of Texas."

"There is not so fair a portion of the earth's surface
warmed by the sun," he wrote of the new land, assuring
his wife he would provide her with "a sweet home." He
added a message for his brother Jack: "to think of nothing
but coming here with us; that if he knew as much about
this country as I already do, he would not be kept from
it." A postscript added: "P.S. Colonel Crockett has just
joined our company."

Twenty-one-year-old Daniel William Cloud, staring
into the flames, was also thinking of the last letter he had
written home, and wondering if he would ever write another. He had remembered, fortunately, to mention the

children, asking his brother to kiss them for him. "We have been travelling 10 weeks and have gone over 2,500 miles—" he had written. "If I were with you I could talk enough to tire you. . . ."

The Texans had eaten with the relish of hard-fighting men; now, with the flames of the fire dying down, they could relax and stretch out for the first time all day. They remembered Jim Bowie, and some of them filed by his cot to pay their respects. He was sitting up now, thanks to the work of Dr. Pollard, but the change in his appearance was startling. He had always looked pale because of his sickness; now he was a sheeted ghost, speaking so softly they could hardly hear. He had two requests to make, knowing how ravaged he was: he insisted upon being isolated for the protection of the others; and he exhorted all his men to give their loyalty to Travis.

For the men who had worshiped him and elected him their leader, the latter request was the most difficult ever made. Many of them turned away to hide their feelings. Of all the men in the Alamo they had looked up only to Bowie and Davy Crockett; and now Bowie, who had fought armies but been struck down by a rolling cannon, was asking them to say good-by.

A few among them knew that the Texans had lost more that day than a good fighter. Bowie, with his Mediterranean mind, was their best liaison man with the Mexican population of Texas, and, had he not been disabled, might have created a countermovement in Santa Anna's own lines. Even his dreams of elegance and prosperity for San Antonio had been based on Mexican models, to make the town another Mexico City. Now his dreams had no potency. It remained for Bowie only to die.

The men had not believed it all day, had not wanted to believe it, that Bowie was not to be with them in the fighting. Now, as they filed by his cot and went out into the starlit courtyard, the evidence was unmistakable. Bowie's loneliness was complete. And Travis, writing in his headquarters room on the other side of the Plaza, was only beginning to feel the weight of single command.

TRAVIS had a gift for words. In writing in his diary and commonplace book he was used to putting his thoughts on paper and, as a young lawyer pleading cases, organizing these thoughts into a coherent pattern. Years of wide reading had supplied the phrases; now the pressure of events supplied a burning eloquence.

He had written often before with the purpose of inflaming to action. Letters to his superiors had been full of eloquent passages asking for help. On January 28, before arriving at San Antonio, he had written Governor Smith:

> Our affairs are gloomy indeed. The people are indifferent. They are worn down and exhausted with war, and in consequence of dissentions between contending and rival chieftains, they had lost all confidence in their government and officers. You have no idea of the exhausted state of the country. Volunteers can no longer be had or relied upon. A speedy organization, classification and draft of the Militia is all that can save us now. A regular army is necessary—but money and MONEY ALONE can raise and equip a regular army.

Two weeks later, writing again to Governor Smith, Travis repeated his plea for help in stronger language:

Santa Anna [has] issued his Proclamation denouncing vengeance against the people of Texas and threatens to exterminate every white man within its limits. This being the Frontier Post nearest the Rio Grande will be the first to be attacked. We are ill prepared for their reception as we have not more than 150 men here and they in a very disorganized state. Yet we are determined to sustain it as long as there is a man left, because we consider death preferable to disgrace....

I fear it is useless to waste argument upon [our countrymen]. THE THUNDER OF THE ENEMY CANNON AND THE POLLUTION OF THEIR WIVES AND DAUGHTERS—THE CRIES OF THEIR FAMISHED CHILDREN AND THE SMOKE OF THEIR BURNING DWELLINGS WILL ONLY AROUSE THEM....

In conclusion, let me assure your Excel'y, that with 200 men, I believe this place can be maintained—and I hope they will be sent us as soon as possible, yet should we receive no reinforcements, I am determined to defend it to the last, and should Bejar fall, your friend will be buried beneath its ruins.

Those had been official reports, made in the line of duty. Now, as he closed the heavy oak door of his headquarters room and went back to his desk, he was preparing to draft a message that would rouse the whole world.

For a moment, as he collected his thoughts, he was glad to be alone in the room he had made his own since coming there three weeks before. From the first he had found the quiet order of the room on the first floor of the long barracks, with its white stone walls, low ceiling, and simple plank table, peaceful and reassuring. It had a plainness and a sturdiness he liked.

The message was taking shape in his mind, and moving the candle for a better light, he picked up the quill pen and began to write. "TO THE PEOPLE OF TEXAS AND ALL AMERICANS IN THE WORLD. . . ." His thoughts raced ahead, faster than his pen could write.

When he had finished he took the message out into the courtyard streaked with the last light of day. There was but one messenger for this message. He summoned Albert Martin. Captain Martin, aged thirty, was a resident of Gonzales, though a native of Tennessee. His horse was extremely fast. Albert Martin had been the hero of the battle of Gonzales last October, when the men of the little town refused to return a five-pound cannon the Mexican government had lent the community for protection against the Indians. Martin, who kept the general store in Gonzales and was a graduate of Captain Partridge's Military School in Connecticut, was the natural leader when Colonel Ugartechea threatened the town. First, he buried the cannon in George W. Davis's peach orchard. Later the men from Gonzales exhumed it and paraded it before the Mexican squad of 100 men, with a pennant on it reading, "Come and Take It." The squad, perhaps because they couldn't read English, took one look at the sign and beat a hasty retreat.

Albert Martin knew the message he was about to deliver now required more caution than aggressiveness. He understood its importance. Waiting for darkness to cover him, he dashed out along the water ditch and safely made his way onto the Gonzales road. On the hard ride, he composed a message of his own. When at last he was safe in Gonzales, he took a pencil and scribbled on the back of Travis's communique: "Since the above was written I have heard a very heavy cannonade during the whole day. I think there must have been an attack on the Alamo. We were short of ammunition when I left. Hurry on all the men you can get in haste. ALBERT MARTIN." Travis's letter had to be shared. Albert Martin passed it on to the next relay, Lancelot Smithers. He, too, penciled on the back his admonition: "I hope that everyone will Rondives [rendez-vous] at Gonzales as soon as possible as these brave soldiers are suffering. Don't neglect them. Powder is very scarce and some should not be delayed one moment. L. SMITHERS." His mission was to carry the message to San Felipe.

When it at last reached its destination Travis's letter was found to read:

TO THE PEOPLE OF TEXAS AND ALL AMERICANS IN THE WORLD—Fellow citizens—& compatriots—I am besieged by a thousand or more of the Mexicans under Santa Anna. —I have sustained a continual bombardment and cannonade for 24 hours & have not lost a man— The enemy has demanded a surrender at discretion, otherwise the garrison are to be put to the sword if the fort is taken—I have answered the demand with a cannon shot, and our flag still waves proudly from the walls—*I shall never surrender or retreat.* Then, I call on you in the name of Liberty, of patriotism & everything dear to the American character, to come to our aid with all dispatch— The enemy is receiving reinforcement daily & will no doubt increase to three or four thousand in four or five days. If this call is neglected, I am determined to sustain myself as long as possible & die like a soldier who never forgets what is due to his own honor & that of his country—VICTORY OR DEATH.

At that point Travis had apparently thought of the men at their evening meal outside, for he added, as an afterthought:

> P.S. The Lord is on our side— When the enemy appeared in sight we had not three bushels of corn— We have since found in deserted houses 80 or 90 bushels & got into the walls 20 or 30 head of beeves.

It was Travis's statement to the world, and one that linked him forever in the public mind with selfless devotion and loyalty.

Meanwhile Albert Martin had started to scour the countryside around Gonzales for men and supplies. He had interpreted correctly what he had heard on his long ride into the DeWitt colony. The Mexicans had begun their serious attack. With all the forces at their command they were shelling the Alamo.

With grenades and grape and canister Santa
Anna gave the Texans in the Alamo a second sleepless
night. He had a further inspiration late in the evening. He
offered the enemy a band concert, the brasses blowing out
their lungs. And he started business briskly next morning,
February 25, at daylight. He ordered the Battalion of
Cazadores to train a battery on the Texans right in front
of the main gate. The Battalion of Ximenes was held in reserve. The watching Texans could not tell whether several
hundred or several thousand Mexican soldiers were ready
to cross the river below the fort. Fire from five-inch
howitzers and a fierce cannonade, designed to obscure the
fording of the stream, did not fool the Texans. But Travis
saw with alarm that the enemy would have good cover,
once they got over the river, behind straw and wooden

117

houses south of the Alamo. Only last night the Texans had quietly sallied forth to bring in supplies of wood from huts near the fortress on the south side. They should have burned down what they had not been able silently to carry away. But theirs was an apprentice army; they were having to learn, by trial and error, in a hurry. Now these huts would give perfect shelter for the Mexicans.

Travis called for volunteers. The operation would have to be performed under enemy fire, and in the clear light of day. He wanted two men, he said, to set fire to the houses 90 or 100 yards in front of the fort. He had hardly spoken when the whole garrison stepped forward. Only two, he repeated; then he chose two wiry reliable youngsters. One was a friend of Jim Bowie, and like Bowie, from Rapides Parish, Louisiana—twenty-four-year-old Charles Despallier. The other was Robert Brown, whom Travis was later to praise that day.

Artillery and rifles prepared to cover the quick sortie of Despallier and Brown. Captain Dickinson directed the cannon fire; Davy Crockett had a sprawl of loaded rifles and his Tennessee Boys beside him. Davy was the champion sharpshooter; in one season back in Tennessee he killed 109 bears. Some of these, of course, may have been in hand-to-hand combat, but Davy Crockett had already staked down his claim to number-one marksmanship. He had picked off the first Mexican on the first day. He didn't imagine the Texans would find enough guns to take care of all the notches he was going to cut. The scoring was just starting. He intended to surpass himself.

Santa Anna had crossed the bridge with the Battalion de Cazadores de Matamoros and had occupied a group of houses near the fort. It was a chance the Texans were eager for. They were expert marksmen, accustomed to bringing down a squirrel a hundred yards away with a shot between the eyes. They mounted the platforms back of their walls and began to fire. A Mexican corporal, exposed, fell dead. A second man on the run fell beside his corporal. The Mexicans fired back but hit no one. This was just the first brush.

The Mexicans were trying only to erect more and nearer batteries, but the Texans thought the real assault was in the making. Some guessed as many as 2,000 of the enemy were in sight; Travis estimated 300. But no one could tell how many were inside the houses. By ten o'clock the battle was raging; the Mexican reserve had crossed the river. The men of the Battalion of Cazadores were trying to establish their battery within pistol shot of the fort. Crockett's men grabbed gun after gun as others stood by to keep them loaded. There was the flash of fire in pan and muzzle, then the inevitable whine. The eight-pounders Captain Dickinson commanded joined in, firing a heavy discharge of grape and canister. At this the Mexican advance halted, as the soldiers raced to take shelter in houses 100 yards away from the Texan fire. Bombardment from both sides remained constant, a discharge of balls that fanned the air with little damage.

The fight raged on till after noontime, when the Mexicans retreated in confusion, dragging their dead and wounded with them. Writing to Sam Houston later, Travis reported enemy losses as heavy, and Texan damage light. Only two or three Texans were "slightly scratched by pieces of rock."

The Texans made their own estimates, figuring the enemy dead as larger even than Travis's count. One report stated that on the third day the 150 Texans had killed between 450 and 600 Mexicans. The Arkansas *Gazette* printed the guess, attributing "this great slaughter" to the "eight guns that every man in the garrison kept loaded by his side."

Meanwhile a cheer went up from the Texans as flames poured from the Mexican houses. Charles Despallier and Robert Brown had done their work well, and now were running back through the flung-open Alamo gates. Travis, his field glass ready, had dispatched them on their arsonist mission while the cannoneers and sharpshooters were creating a diversion. The two youths zigzagged across the no man's land between the fort and the enemy entrenchment south of it, gained the protection of the front house in the thin line of small dwellings, and set fire to it and others nearby. They raced back into the Alamo unscathed, as the Mexican fusillade bit at their heels and whined around them. It was a daring maneuver. Their luck was perfect. An immense roar of relief greeted their safe return. Breathing harder than they had ever breathed before, they stretched out a moment on the ground near Crockett's stockade.

They had done more for William Barret Travis than they knew. He knew it, and so did Davy Crockett. They had proved their own courage, but they also had proved Travis as commander. If anybody had doubted these men would fight for William Barret Travis as they would for Jim Bowie, such persons could now recant.

Crockett, who knew how much was at stake, had covered all points of attack, spurring the men on to do not only their duty but their best. Travis noticed and was grateful. He returned to his headquarters room and with a gesture now growing into a habit he reached for paper and pen to report to General Sam Houston on the behavior of his men under fire.

After praising Crockett and Dickinson and the two youngsters, Travis was jubilant at the quality his men had revealed. He declared the Alamo garrison had "undaunted heroism." And then he reminded his commander again of their desperate need for help. He hoped for reinforcements in a day or two, but said he would hold out "to the last extremity."

He closed his report: "Do hasten aid on to me as rapidly as possible, from the superior number of the enemy, it will be impossible for us to keep them out much longer. If they overpower us, we fall a sacrifice at the shrine of our country, and we hope posterity and our country will do our memory justice. Give me help, oh my Country! Victory or Death!"

Santa Anna did not mean to be kept out very long. Nor did he mean to let his orders go unexecuted. As soon as dark lent its aid, the battalions again began the installation of batteries, a couple of howitzers—one five-and-a-half-inch and the other eight- and two long nine-pounders. This time the cover of night was beneficial. Still protected by some standing *jacales* between the Alamo and the bridge on the southwest side, the Mexicans set up their closest battery to date, only 300 yards away from the entrance port. Less ambitiously, but still closing in the ring, they established another a thousand yards southeast, by the old powder house. To cut off retreat toward the settlements and to intercept reinforcements, Santa Anna posted his cavalry on the Gonzales road to the east. The trap was almost set.

The Texans were profiting from the dark too, moving in noiselessly to burn down the houses that had served as enemy barricade. A sudden norther had blown up and by nine o'clock the temperature had dropped thirty degrees. The whistling wind sliced through their buckskin breeches and made the prospect of fire, no matter how dangerous to set, seem enticing. The small detail got to the low structures without being seen and started their fires on the inside, to let another moment or so of darkness cover their retreat. The blaze that shot up, fanned by the wind, blinded them a moment but hid them from sight.

For a while a blazing sheet of red-yellow flame curtained the Alamo from the enemy quartered on the far side of the river, the northern blast blowing the smoke away from both camps. A spatter of Mexican fusillade stippled the ground around the incendiaries, and they sprinted back to the walls, yelling out the password yards away. The gates were opened wide and a volley greeted their safe return. Were they all there? A swift roll call was made and the breathing eased. Every man had made it back. They hurried to the ramps to admire the bonfire they had made. With this gale there wouldn't even be any smoke left by morning.

They suddenly felt empty, but not tired. Travis's praise had lifted their weariness. If it had not been so cold, they might have asked Davy Crockett to get out his fiddle and sing some of his songs, or tell some of his stories about how he got to Little Rock on the way to Texas riding a catamount and with a bear under each arm and left town the same way. Or how he decided to come to Texas because the soil was so rich, if you planted a crowbar at night it'd sprout ten-penny nails before morning. But no stories now. It took all the attention they had just to keep from freezing. As though Santa Anna needed help from the weather to keep them from sleeping.

MANY A MAN that night must once again have asked himself: "What am I doing here?" It was easy and natural to wonder why they had come to Texas. They often talked about it. A favorite answer, and a good one, concerned the seventeen-year-old lad back in Kentucky who rolled up his clothing, got on his horse, hung his gun over the saddle bow, and rode forth to tell his neighbors good-by.

"But, why?" they wanted to know. "Why are you goin' off to Texas?"

Their ignorance baffled him. It was perfectly clear, as he told them, "Why? Why, I'm a-goin' to Texas to fight for my rights!"

Often it had been as clear and as irrational as that. And yet the answer made a kind of sense. One American right was to go where you pleased unhindered. Wherever a horse could take you, no one could block your way. That was how David Crockett had felt when the voters of Tennessee, after electing him as their representative twice, put a rival in Congress. Disgusted as well as insulted, Davy told his former constituents: "You-all can go to hell and I'm a-going to Texas!"

Davy Crockett was nearer the temperament of most of the men in the Alamo than any of the other leaders. They loved Bowie for his daring and for the obvious fact that the man didn't know what fear was; they came to admire Travis. Bonham was by nature a patrician, a man apart. But in Crockett they found the flavor of frontier life.

In their minds they saw him not riding his catamount into Little Rock, a bear under each arm, but as a giant straddling the Alamo, a giant part horse and part alligator, holding a Mexican captured and wiggling in each palm. When he opened his mouth, he made thunder. When he flashed his eyes in anger, there was lightning. And if he were crossed in anything he made the earth quake.

Before the siege, he had made the best speeches in the Plaza, and they had a passion for speechifying; he made the best toddies, crushing into a little water a lump of sugar with a knife or his finger and mixing it with barefoot rum; his presence at the table gave the meal a flourish. Davy had been there only fifteen days before Santa Anna's arrival, but they had been lively days. Santa Anna had merely extended Davy's repertory. He had been cracking jokes about him ever since. But each day they grew less funny.

Charles Despallier might have been able to give another reason for coming to Texas. In him was that unknown quality that made the cowboy a national myth.

Despallier was a good-looking boy, in love with guns, which he handled with steady hands. He loved horses, too. For young men who felt at home in the saddle, Texas, with its herds of wild horses and cattle roaming the plains after their introduction by the Spanish *conquistadores*, was a paradise. In Europe the man on horseback had traditionally been an aristocrat—a "*caballero*," a "chevalier," a "cavalier." In the New World you were on horseback because you loved the sense of power that rose from the horse's body into your own. You loved the speed of motion as the air swept cool over the sides of your ears, the music of the hooves striking sparks from rocks in the road, the deep breathing of this superb animal that could carry you fifty or sixty miles in a day.

But Charles Despallier's world had now grown smaller. Till help came from Houston and the men at Goliad, this three-acre square of limestone and adobe buildings hemmed him in. Any motion this fourth morning of the siege was limited to speeding bullets. As day broke, the fires were fed again and the Texans ate for breakfast what they ate for lunch and supper too: corn and beef.

As they looked down from a parapet on the outer defense walls, the men shared the nostalgia of Charles Despallier. Never before had the town of San Antonio, set down like a pearl in its cup-shaped valley, looked so satisfying. The norther had cleansed the sky and the air to a Mediterranean blue. The hand-hewn stone buildings and the low adobe houses caught the light and filled the spaces between the two adjoining plazas and the San Fernando Church with a dazzling shine. The giant pecans and cypresses and the gnarled cottonwoods along the river and its *acequias* reflected the light in their thrust of intricate branches on the air.

The bell tolling from the church tower floated its sound amid the explosions of cannonade and the shatter of muskets. The men who could no longer stroll down those streets and halt at the *cantina* for talk and drink became aware of an affection for the town they had never troubled consciously to note before.

For young Charles Despallier, as for others here, San Antonio, though only a remote outpost at the edge of advancing American dominion, was an ancient town and a metropolis. It was ancient because it dated from 1718—a respectable age as things in North America went. And it was a metropolis because of the zestful spirit the transplanted Europeans had brought to it. Fiestas were frequent and San Antonio had a reputation for the beauty of its daughters. After all, His Catholic Majesty had founded this tiny metropolis, so isolated in the wilderness and 1,200 miles from its mother city in Mexico, with the intent to make it a symbol of Spain. Against their will Philip V had transported a number of the best families from the Canary Islands to create this city whose name and whose river would honor Saint Anthony.

On fine days that winter, before Santa Anna came, when the brimming sun forecast the broiling summer, Charles Despallier had ridden into the bare, brown countryside to inspect the land he would choose when Santa Anna had been directed, like Cós, to the other side of the Rio Grande. He would be rich in land if Texas won. The provisional government promised handsome rewards for volunteers: "two square miles of land, a barony in the old country."

The volunteers at the Alamo knew soils and crops. Most of them came from the Old South, from rich farm lands far more wooded and picturesque than these. Here they looked out on waves of endless grass, now the color of straw, and the eye never halted till it reached the rimless flat horizon that gave them the feeling they were on the top of the world. Some day, these Texans told each other, they would ride to their own *rancherias*, organizing their own cattle kingdoms and wondering which was a better sight, mesquite or green magnolia.

Some preferred to farm as they had back home. But the *rancherias* they rode by seemed perfect for the region. It was ranching that lured twenty-one-year-old Daniel William Cloud of Kentucky. From the herds of wild cattle roaming the prairies, a man could set himself up easily as a rancher, with a little farm on the side. Daniel Cloud's hungers were not all for land and adventure. Half the charm of the outlying ranches was in their compact, serene adobe houses, the walls hung with drying strings of red and yellow peppers, and the neat gardens outside thriving with tomato vines, figs, squash, onions, garlic and odd-looking greens for which the Texans had no names. There were berries, wild mustang grapevines, and nuts, the pecan trees reaching impressive height; and every ranch had its bees, whose honey was served the visiting young *caballeros* —on frijoles or beans, often mixed with onions as a sauce. Then there were novel items the Texans ate and guessed must be okra (it was young shoots of cactus plants) or water cress (it was *verdaloga*) or a kind of cabbage (which was *quelito*).

On the day after Christmas, Daniel Cloud had written his brother:

> The reason for our pushing further on must now be told, and as it is a master one, it will suffice without mention of any other. Ever since Texas unfurled the banner of freedom and commenced a warfare for "Liberty or Death," our hearts have been enlisted in her behalf.... If we succeed, the country is ours: It is immense in extent and fertile in soil and will amply reward all our toils. If we fail, death in the cause of liberty and humanity is not cause for shuddering.

On their Texas ranches or farms, these young Texans, proud in their victory, would listen to the shrill beat of the locusts and feel at one with the rhythm of the rolling earth. They felt its stir in their legs every time they walked over the ground. They would live outdoors, not in—the way Davy Crockett lived his life.

GEORGE WASHINGTON was about to begin his first term as president when Davy Crockett was born. Davy's ancestors were high-born Irish; Davy's first wife was said to be a direct descendant of Macbeth, King of Scotland. His father had fought alongside the unprofessional soldiers of Washington's first army, farmers who like the Texans could peg a squirrel fifty yards away.

Davy Crockett, like Travis, Bowie, and Bonham, grew up in a world in which the American revolution was the greatest single event in all history. When he came to Texas at the age of fifty—after a career on the frontier and in Congress—it was inevitable that he would see the comparison between the Texas Revolution and the events of 1776.

The Texan army was small, but so was Washington's. During the winter at Valley Forge, the number of effectives commanded by Washington dropped to around 3,000. The Texans had routed General Cós with an army of 1,000. In leaving after the victory to plant their spring corn they were also doing what the farmers at Lexington had done.

Similarly, in rebelling against Santa Anna's military dictatorship, they were only following the thirteen original colonies in their revolt against absentee ownership and taxation without representation. The colonists had made

The Fall of the Alamo, by Theodore Gentilz (1844). The original painting has been destroyed. (Courtesy, Library of the Daughters of the Republic of Texas at the Alamo)

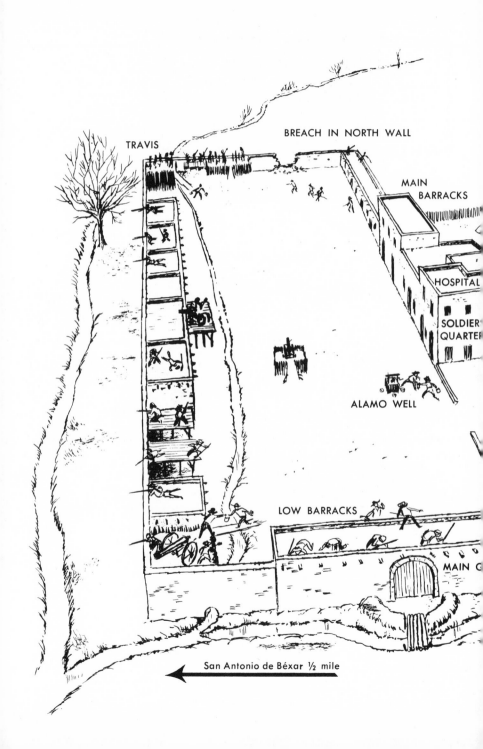

TRAVIS

BREACH IN NORTH WALL

MAIN
BARRACKS

HOSPITAL

SOLDIER'
QUARTER

ALAMO WELL

LOW BARRACKS

MAIN G

San Antonio de Béxar ½ mile

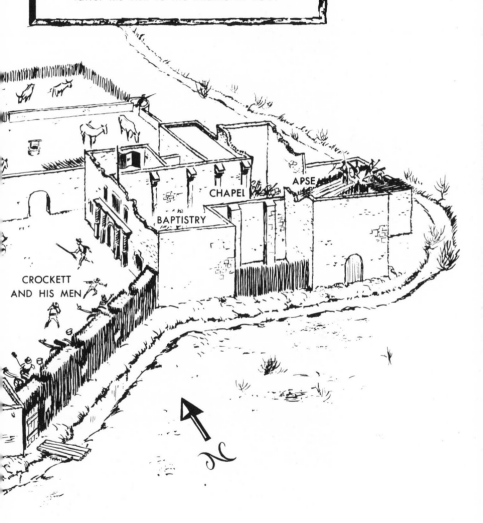

THE ALAMO UNDER FIRE

based on sketches by Lt. J. Edmund Blake in 1845 and Lt. Edward Everett in 1846 and on the map drawn by Capt. R. M. Potter after his visit to the Alamo in 1841

APSE

CHAPEL

BAPTISTRY

CROCKETT AND HIS MEN

William Barret Travis, from an idealized composite portrait by
H. A. McArdle. (Courtesy, Library of the Daughters of the
Republic of Texas at the Alamo)

General Antonio Lopez de Santa Anna at the time of the
Mexican War.

James Bowie, by Benjamin West. This is one of the few portraits
of Bowie in existence. (Courtesy, Library of the Daughters of
the Republic of Texas at the Alamo)

Davy Crockett, by John Gadsby Chapman. (Courtesy, the
Alamo)

Davy Crockett's Last Stand, by Robert Onderdonk (1903).
(Courtesy, Texas Governor's Mansion)

This imaginative engraving of the Alamo during the Civil War appeared in *Harper's Weekly*, March 23, 1861. (Courtesy, Special Collections, Texas A&M University Library)

The Alamo Chapel as it looks today after restoration. (Courtesy, Library of the Daughters of the Republic of Texas at the Alamo)

Texas the fastest-growing and most prosperous agricultural province of Mexico, and were untaxed for seven years. When they made the land pay off, the Mexican government—seated at far-off Mexico City, six weeks away by horse—had promptly initiated its customs duties and taxes and quartered soldiers among them, some of them ex-convicts. Texas was joined in statehood with Coahuila, and in their joint state legislature had only one vote out of a dozen, later three. The worst blow had been Santa Anna's destruction of even this inadequate legislature—along with the National Congress—and the creation of an onerous personal dictatorship. The Texans had only one choice: to follow the example of their fathers and forefathers.

Davy Crockett had started his rebellion early. At the age of twelve he ran away from his home at Limestone Springs in eastern Tennessee—where his roving father settled after soldiering in the American Revolution—because his father put him in school and took the teacher's side against him. The youth had not been to school before; he stayed for four days, then left for three years. He worked at odd jobs, chiefly as a drover, until he realized at fifteen he was almost grown without "knowing a letter in the book." Returning home, he found his father "head over heels in debt." By now father and son both had learned a lesson about each other. John Crockett made a deal with his independent son: If Davy would work off one of his father's debts, John Crockett would never again treat him as a minor. Davy carried out the bargain, then worked another six months of his own choice and without telling his father to clear another of his father's debts. This time he learned another lesson in the hardest possible way.

The second creditor was a Quaker with a young niece, lovely and with some education. She spurned the illiterate Crockett, and his feelings were so hurt he decided to go back to school. The Quaker agreed to let Davy work part time, go to school the other. This six months was all the formal schooling of the man who later signed his name to a series of memorable books, whether he really wrote them or spoke the material to scriveners better trained, but no more intelligent, than he. His experience in Congress and other public office turned him into a self-educated man. He was even able to interest the girls, though his training came too late to help him win the Quaker's niece or her successor, a girl who repaid his love by jilting him.

With Davy, third time was charm. Now eighteen and the best shot in the country, he fell in love with an Irish girl, Polly Finley. This time he planned to make sure of success by a system of "close courtship," so close no rival had a chance to get near the girl. But it was not his rivals or his ignorance that thwarted him; it was the reluctance of Polly's parents. Ultimately they were won over by Polly's stubborn insistence, and even contributed to the young couple's endowment two cows and calves, which allowed Davy, who had a horse, to set up as a farmer.

"Having gotten my wife," Davy later said, "I thought I was completely made up, and needed nothing more in the whole world. But I soon found this was all a mistake —for now having a wife, I wanted everything else; and, worse than all, I had nothing to give for it." By 1812 he was seeking adventure again, this time with General Andrew Jackson—a man he came later and unluckily to loathe—in the bloody war against the Creek Indians in Florida. It was a primitive-type war on both sides. Davy says he once ate some potatoes seared in the grease of a burned Creek warrior's body.

When Polly Finley died soon after the 1812 campaign, Davy Crockett married the widow of a soldier lost in the Creek War. Although, as Davy said, she owned a "snug little farm and lived quite comfortably," they shortly moved westward into wilderness country where civil law had still to be established. Davy Crockett was a charmer. He had merely to open his mouth and the glib flow of picturesque and canny speech spellbound his listeners. For him politics was a career as easy as singing is to a born tenor. He became a magistrate in the newly organized settlement in the wilderness, knowing nothing about law, save for "natural law." Davy was such a success he presently ran for the legislature and discovered his skills as a campaigner. With ease he won two terms in the state legislature. He was getting an education fast, learning the meaning of "judiciary reform," the kind of term that completely baffled him when he first had to talk politics with people already won over by his charm.

He had the common sense, however, to keep his new learning private rather than to parade it. What people liked in him was his honesty, his forthrightness, his shrewd simplicity. This core of naturalness reassured them. Otherwise they would have, in the boredom of frontier life, relished his monkeyshines and his jokes but feared him as a man too clever to be true.

He was clever all right, but he was true, too. If not, he would never have hurt his political chances by his forthright opposition to Andrew Jackson's Indian Bill. Jackson's spoils system insured Crockett's defeat for his third term in the state legislature, but this failure was offset by Crockett's national acclaim as an anti-Jackson man. Politicians from the North exploited this backwoods rebel against the equally backwoods Jackson. Davy got himself elected to Congress, then for a second term. Washington prepared to enjoy itself. In frontier outfit, Crockett became the national topic of conversation, a curious freak who fed intuitively and knowingly the people's amusement. He was funny when he proposed abolishing West Point Military Academy to divide any government bounty among the poor and downtrodden, instead of fostering institutions for the wealthy and powerful. But he was fearless in his basic beliefs: "I would vote to go through any gentleman's estate with a road or a canal if it was for the good of the whole union, and I do not believe I will ever give up this doctrine."

To President Jackson, who made the spoils system nationally acceptable, this was heresy. In Tennessee he aided in the thorough defeat of Crockett's fourth campaign for the Congress. It was then Davy decided his constituents could go to hell—he was going to Texas.

But his rage soon gave way to the strongest instinct in him, the need to treat life playfully. Texas was a new game, or rather, a new setting for the basic American experience: colonization, prosperous settlement, revolt in favor of independence. There was as much land available in Texas as there was sky. It cost 12½ cents an acre. Back in 1820, land in the United States had cost $1.25 an acre if bought in the government's public domain. And the American government was asking cash payments for its land. But in Texas, you could even work out the down payment from your first crops.

Two months after his defeat in 1835 Davy Crockett

wrote his brother-in-law, George Patton of Swannanoa, North Carolina:

> Weakley County Tennessee
> Octr 31st 1835
>
> Dear Brother
> I have concluded to drop you a line the whole Connection is well and I am on the eve of starting to the Texes —on tomorrow morning mySelf Abner Burgin [another brother-in-law] and Lindsy K. Tinkle & our Nephew William Patton from the Lowar Country this will make our Company we will go through Arkinsaw and I want to explore the Texes well before I return....
>
> David Crockett

The letter says nothing of the Texas journey as an urge to join the fight against Santa Anna. Nor does it mention his wife and children, whom he left behind but intended to send for later. His first Texas letter—and his last—from Nacogdoches, dated January 9, 1836, is eloquent about Texas independence. He writes his son and daughter a joint letter to assure them he is in high spirits and fine health—and "I must say as to What I have seen of Texas, it is the garden spot of the world ... good land, plenty of timber, good mill streams, good range, clear water & every appearance of health—game a plenty. It is in the pass where the buffalo passes from the north to south and back twice a year and bees and honey a plenty."

He adds without vanity that the citizens of Nacogdoches fired a cannon to welcome him, that he had been "received by everybody with open arms of friendship," that the ladies have invited him to dinners. The heart of his letter is: "I have taken the oath of the government and have enrolled my name as a volunteer for six months, and will set out for the Rio Grande in a few days with the volunteers of the U.S. . . . I had rather be in my present situation than to be elected to a seat in Congress for life. I am in great hopes of making a fortune for myself and family bad as has been my prospects."

As he set out for the Alamo, he added a last sentence to his children: "I hope you will do the best you can and I will do the same, do not be uneasy about me I am with my friends. . . . Your affectionate father, Farewell, DAVID CROCKETT."

Davy did take the oath of allegiance to the Texan government, but not so simply as he records in this letter. His staunch republican sentiments were manifest again: The oath required one to swear "true allegiance to the provisional government of Texas, or any future government that may be hereafter declared. . . ." Davy refused to sign this version, contending that the future government might be despotic. The colonel in charge inserted the word "republican" between the words "future" and "government," and Davy signed with a flourish.

This letter reveals something else significant. Davy planned to make a fortune in Texas; he suggests that he plans to be a land agent. Chiefly, he became a volunteer in the Texan army so that he might be elected to the Constitutional Convention of the Texans. He writes: "I have but little doubt of being elected a member to form a constitution for this province." His political career was about to have a spectacular rebirth. From the Presidency of Texas . . . on to the White House? Or like young Daniel William Cloud of Kentucky, a simple free life in the open air?

THE TEXANS in the Alamo did not know it but one of their shots had nearly nicked *El Presidente* the day before. He was still nursing his anger. Santa Anna, who had defeated the army he most admired in history, the Spanish, could have nothing but scorn for these farmers and hunters who dared not only to reject his laws but to subjugate his chief city in Texas and humiliate his army. His reputation before world opinion required him to inflict a dramatic punishment—he who called himself "the Napoleon of the West."

His contempt was really for the land of Texas too. His government had never been able to move in settlers here from the beautiful central plateau of Mexico. It took simple-minded backwoodsmen to risk their lives for such a flat land, broiling, except when northers struck, under the sun. By comparison, Santa Anna's own estate at *Manga de Clavo* was an empire, a dominion of some of the most favored landscape and soil on the continent. Sheltered by overhanging mountains on the north, six thousand feet above sea level, it offered in abundance flowers and forest and game and fruits, not to mention poppies for his opium. If Santa Anna could have glimpsed the simple dreams of such Texans as Daniel Cloud and Charles Despallier, he would have snorted.

When he thought of Mexico City and all its splendor, an ache for luxury swept over him. This was a sorry place to fight for. He was glad now he had brought along the cart of fighting cocks. A cock fight would be distracting, a memory of Mexico.

While contempt is the occupational disease of the champion, it is often buttressed by real superiorities. This was true of Santa Anna. At the age of nineteen—the same year Davy Crockett was fighting alongside Andrew Jackson in Florida—he was already proving his battle skill by exterminating Indians under General Arredondo. He had won a colonelcy, by successive promotions, at the age of twenty-nine. He had fought almost as long as Napoleon; seven years ago, he had turned back Spain from its futile attempt to reconquer Mexico. Seven months ago in Zacatecas, in May of 1835, he had crushed with unbelievable cruelty the last remaining opposition to his overthrow of the constitution save one—these Texans now before him, most of them firing a gun at human beings for the first time, styling themselves colonels and majors, confronting him with an army that didn't seem to have one private in it. The soldier who had waited thirteen years for a colonelcy could only smile. A man without a title in Texas was clearly lacking in imagination.

Santa Anna's actions the previous May should have been a warning to the Texans. He had been demoniacal to his own people in Zacatecas; the Texans could expect the same. Through his consuls and minister in Washington he had warned America. Any "foreigners" fighting on Texas soil, or any Americans sending money or supplies into Texas, would be executed as public enemies. He was not fighting soldiers but pirates, men without a country.

His country—and his vanity was such that he regarded it as "his" country—held land expanses north and west of Texas that made Mexico equal in size to the United States. His capital was the biggest city in the hemisphere, having a population of 150,000 in 1821 to New York's 120,000. It was also the richest. The Spaniards had shipped out of Mexico in three centuries more than eight billion dollars of gold and silver.

Silver, not gold, seemed to him the symbol of Mexico City. It was everywhere. Silver adorned the cavaliers as well as their mounts. Silver bells and spikes and buttons hung from hats, jackets, leather blankets and saddles, bridles, and rowels. The late afternoon parades on the Paseo, when the high-born and privileged ladies appeared in their gilt carriages and dresses of Chinese silks, bespoke a life of leisure and wealth—for the ruling class, at any rate. England's first emissary to Mexico said the grandeur in the capital surpassed that of Rome. The Scottish-born Madame Calderon de la Barca, wife of the Spanish ambassador, was particularly impressed by it, as was Missouri-bred Stephen F. Austin, who wrote his brother, "This city is truly a magnificent one. . . ."

There was grandeur all over Mexico in the mountainous landscapes white-dotted with lonely, magnificent haciendas, but life in the capital was the best the hemisphere offered. A population instinctively artistic, ready to spurn the practical in favor of the dramatic, hailed Santa Anna as the most important man in Mexico. He could always make a rational case for his side. After espousing republicanism, then abandoning it, he claimed that Mexico —with no tradition of self-government—was not ready for democracy. Mexico needed a benevolent despot or it would dissolve into anarchy.

He had thoroughly demonstrated his scorn for Texans in his treatment of Stephen F. Austin. Austin had journeyed to Mexico City in 1833 to present a plan for separate statehood, a plan largely authored by Sam Houston. When he saw he was being delayed in the capital as a hostage against Texas revolt, Austin imprudently wrote back for the Texans to organize their separate state without waiting for permission. His letter was seized, and he languished—with no company but a prison rat and without books to read or paper to write on—in a cell of the Inquisition, later in easier imprisonment, until the autumn of 1835.

By this torture of one man Santa Anna hoped to teach all insurgent Texans a lesson. After eighteen months' imprisonment Austin was released in the belief that his return to Texas would spread terror and intimidation and that he would advise submission.

This misjudgment of so remarkable a man as Stephen F. Austin was a grave error on Santa Anna's part. From his childhood in Virginia and the Spanish territory of Louisiana, in Missouri, through his maturing in Arkansas and in New Orleans, Stephen F. Austin had mingled with the mixed populations of frontier America. A sensitive mind and a legal one, Austin early acquired an almost Spanish love of punctilio, an instinctive sympathy for appearance and form which he revealed in discarding, at an early date, frontier buckskin for the elegant clothing of New Orleans.

With his sense of tact, Austin charmed the people with whom he and his father had cast their lot. The Mexicans knew at once that he was a man of honor. Time after time they accorded him instant respect, by that quick response in which men appreciate each other's character on sight. Austin had patience and a diplomatic presence. The first Mexican officials who saw him in Texas, minor officials in a remote province far from the rulers in Mexico City, recognized him as a reliable and thoughtful man, and sent advance word to San Antonio to insure that Austin and the sixteen "men of consequence" with him should be received properly by Governor Martínez. The governor was particularly cordial. Until the inevitable explosion of the Texan colonists against the Mexican government, Austin was uniformly correct, universally admired. And despite all the heartbreaking delays and rebuffs he met in Mexico City, Austin's severest judgment was not against Santa Anna but against his own compatriot, Colonel Anthony Butler, whom Andrew Jackson sent to Mexico City to buy Texas for the United States. Butler tried to bribe everybody. When Mexico asked his recall, he blamed Austin for foiling him—as he may well have done. Austin called him "the most base man I have ever met."

If Santa Anna thought all Americans were like Butler, Americans thought all Mexicans like Santa Anna. To Texans, Santa Anna was simply a villain. Villain he was, but not a simple one. When he had first pronounced for a "free and independent Mexico" in 1821, just as the Texans were starting to colonize the state, they thought any government he headed would be first cousin to the democracies born of the French and American revolutions.

Thinking of Mexico City on this morning of February 26, how could General Santa Anna fail to hate Béxar and the country his army had traversed to get here? The men who had died on the march from Saltillo, the casualties among the animals, the abandoning of supplies that left his army on half rations in weather every bit as bad as even the pessimists had predicted—for all this he blamed the land. Santa Anna himself was nearly a casualty from the amoebic dysentery which plagued him all his life. All this trouble, despite the thorough provisioning of the 1,800 pack mules, 300 two-wheel carts, and fifty or more four-wheel wagons. Not even all this could handle the hauling.

Supplies were still waiting at Monclova till other transport could be assembled.

Now he was in Béxar, and he had already begun major maneuvers. He remembered with pride his moves of the previous night.

He had blockaded escape from the Alamo. The exit to the east, to the colonies and to colleagues, had been open to the Texans for the first two days without any real danger. Had they wanted to escape, had they changed their minds about the wisdom of delaying Santa Anna or waiting for reinforcements, they could have readily got away.

But not after the fourth day of the siege. By posting cavalry on the hills east of the Alamo blocking the Gonzales Road, Santa Anna had rendered difficult not merely escape, but likewise approach.

FOR THE FIRST TIME, Travis and Crockett and the other officers at the Alamo doubted their confidence when they saw in the morning light of February 26—a raw and bitterly cold morning—that entrance from Goliad would not benefit from surprise.

By now Charles Despallier and Daniel Cloud and the others were accustomed to missing sleep. The Texans did not have enough men to patrol the walls in relays or in shifts. They had to take what catnaps and brief siestas a staggered system of rest periods allowed. They slept at their posts along the walls, guns ready and loaded. Sleep was a luxury—but who wanted to sleep when bonfires and sudden northers and enemy maneuvering provided such excitements? Sleep could wait until reinforcements arrived.

They observed that Travis was briefing another courier. This made almost a dozen messengers already dispatched. Dr. John Sutherland and John W. Smith had gone out the afternoon the Mexican army entered the town. Before them, Travis had sent out several townspeople and some army men. Sam Maverick—on his way to serve at the Independence Convention—had ridden by the Alamo just after the Texans had assembled there. The men had heard him talk with Travis as he stood on the wall. Travis had told him to ride on to Gonzales and to spread the word. From his saddle, Maverick had called up that he would find men and supplies. Not long after, Travis had sent out Captain Philip Dimitt and merchant Nat Lewis.

Two other couriers had left the fort that first afternoon behind Sutherland and Smith. Just about the time Jim Bonham rode in from Goliad, Travis sent another message straight to Fannin, by a young man named Johnson. He also sent Lancelot Smithers, to whom Albert Martin had delivered his "message to the world." Benjamin Highsmith, on the same day, was dispatched to Fannin, and John Baylor went on the third day, with the report to Houston. Thus they had gone—Maverick, Sutherland, Smith, Dimitt, Lewis, Johnson, Highsmith, Baylor—to Gonzales and Goliad, carrying Travis's hopes and pleas. And now Travis was signaling the outside world again.

Surely reinforcements were on the way by now. The men strained to hear the echo of hooves beating the ground. All they heard was gun fire.

9

On the fifth day of the siege, February 27, the lack of news began to prey on the Texans' minds. They were isolated from the outside world in the most helpless sort of way: their hopes led them to picture Fannin en route, Sam Houston riding west at the head of unnumbered volunteers, all the messengers hastening back with men and provisions in tow. There was no way to verify these images that chased across their minds. They wanted news. Davy Crockett told Mrs. Dickinson: "I'd rather go through these gates and shoot it out with the Mexicans beyond these walls; I hate to be hemmed in." Skepticism and doubt began to rise. If just one messenger returned to say help was on the way, their uncertainty would vanish. Goliad was only four days' foot march from the Alamo. If the couriers sent out on the 23rd got there, they ought to be

142

riding back with news by now. Any news, just so it was a fact and not a dream. Travis stared at the flaking ancient whitewash on his room's walls. He was calculating time lapse too. Each morning, the hopeful tomorrow of the night before had become the emptiness of today.

Why, Travis was wondering, didn't Fannin come? Why didn't Governor Smith and Sam Houston send reinforcements? For five days the men in the Alamo had suppressed the despair that reality kept bringing to their minds. Now they were running short of powder.

The disadvantages of the Alamo as a fortress were also beginning to loom as grim realities. The outer walls, three feet thick, were not strong enough to withstand prolonged bombardment, nor high enough to discourage scaling. There were no bastions and, except for the *acequias*, no moats or ditches. There were not even loopholes to fire through; riflemen firing over the outer wall had to stand momentarily with head and shoulders exposed.

Nor was their armament sufficient. A battery of three twelve-pounders in the apse of the chapel, four more in the courtyard outside, two protecting the porte-cochere on the south, the eighteen-pounder at the southern end of the west wall—these, together with the three in the north and the one twelve-pounder in the center of the western wall, made a total of fourteen guns, none of them of the calibre a fort this size needed. Only one pointed east.

Obviously the fort could not stand by means of its own defenses. Reinforcements *must* come.

In his fever of concern, Travis summoned the man whose company and friendship helped him the most. Since no scout had returned with aid, it might be that none had made it through the enemy lines. Jim Bonham could make it. Much as he had hated seeing Bonham return empty-handed the first day of the siege, Travis had been more than grateful for his presence inside the fort. He was ready now, because of the urgency of the situation, to deprive himself of the strengthening presence of his boyhood friend.

The Mexican army was getting reinforcements steadily. Their cannonade had grown and sounded twice as loud now that the Texans were not firing back. Travis was conserving his supply of balls and shot and scrap iron and cut-up iron chains. But the enemy fire was so constant the men had to move within the walls' open spaces on the run. No Texan had yet been hit.

The men standing watch on the north wall blew on their chilled fingers, cold from the metal barrels of the guns, cold from the north wind. Then they saw target.

A small Mexican detail, unaware of the existence of a well inside the Alamo walls, was attempting to cut off the Texan water supply. The maneuver was not a difficult one, the only problem being to evade the accuracy of the long rifles. The water ditches flowing on the east and the west side of the fortress sluiced off from the river. The ditch on the west forked, and flowed a tributary through the Alamo compound. In plain sight, the Mexican detail was trying to dam it up with logs and timber, or at least to thin the supply to a trickle. They worked without cover, but the Mexican batteries were firing balls so fast the Texans hardly dared raise their heads to take aim.

It was a brave attempt but Texan marksmanship was good. One, two, three Mexicans—all probably volunteers for this risky assignment—went down in a hurry. As their comrades pulled them aside, two more fell. The attempt

was abandoned as suddenly as it started; the water kept
flowing clear. The Texans, in jubilation and as though they
needed it, filled skin-bags and tubs.

No reinforcements yet, but water, plenty of water.

When Bonham entered the doorway of the room
that served Travis as headquarters, the two men seemed
to crowd the low-ceilinged place. Both were over six feet
tall, both commanding in presence.

Though they did not know it, they were distant kin
by marriage. Many Texans thought they looked like
brothers, despite Travis's curly auburn hair and Bonham's
wavy black hair. Both were strikingly handsome and
both well aware of their native gifts. As boys, whose
families lived five miles apart in the Edgefield District of
South Carolina, they had gone to school together, spent
their summers fishing, hunting, and riding. When Travis
was twelve, his family had moved to Alabama, but he and
Bonham had kept their friendship alive by letters. They
had shared ambitions, vaguely hoping to build political
careers on apprenticeships at law.

Both Travis and Bonham were rebels, of a special sort,
from birth. They were perfectionists, rebelling against the
half-a-loaf that life offers those who dream best. Both were
—inevitably perhaps—unfortunate or unhappy in love.

In 1830, at the age of twenty-three Bonham set up a
law office at Pendleton, South Carolina. He promptly revealed his rebellious and chivalric nature, particularly in
what is doubtless his most famous case.

His client was a lady greatly respected in the community. When Bonham judged that she had been insulted
by a remark of the other lawyer, he promptly waylaid this
opponent and single-handedly tossed him out of the court-

room. The judge called this violent and irregular, and was attempting to rebuke the protector of southern womanhood, when Bonham stopped him in his tracks: "Judge, if you carry on like that, I'll have to tweak your nose." The judge condemned Bonham for contempt of court. Bonham was not going to pay a fine when he had merely been doing his duty; he served his sentence in jail. The ladies brought him southern-fried chicken every day, and lined the walls of his cell with freshly cut flowers.

Bonham did not have the same success with ladies in the singular as in the plural. The one he most wanted belonged to someone else, and Bonham transferred his affections not to another girl but to another community. He must get his humiliation out of sight. In 1834 he moved his law practice to Montgomery, Alabama. He had acquired the title of colonel before leaving South Carolina, having had that rank as aide on the staff of Governor James Hamilton in the excitement over nullification in 1832. He had also briefly commanded a company of artillery at Charleston, when the possibility loomed of battle with the national government. Henry Clay's compromise put an end to that.

A year after Bonham reached Montgomery, he got a letter from Travis, who had left for Texas three years before. Travis's letter ended, after much praise of the land, with the sentence, "Stirring times are afoot here; come out to Texas and take a hand in affairs."

Bonham was twenty-eight and life had not given him as much as he hoped. He decided to try Texas. First he had to ride back to South Carolina to tell his mother good-by and settle his affairs. His brother supplied him with the necessary money despite a premonition that he was doing the wrong thing. And in January, 1836, the following announcement appeared in the *Texas Telegraph and Register*, published at San Felipe de Austin:

LAW NOTICE:
  The subscriber will open a law office in Brazoria, to receive such business as he may be favored with in his profession. He has with him licenses to practice law in South Carolina and Alabama of the United States of the North.

  JAMES B. BONHAM

  Bonham was to have little opportunity to practice law, however. Soon after his arrival he was helping Travis operate the Texas recruiting service. Commissioned a lieutenant of cavalry, Bonham quickly won the admiration of Sam Houston, who recommended him to the Council—with Houston's usual lack of success with that fractious group—to be a major. When Jim Bowie went to the Alamo on January 17, bearing Sam Houston's orders to "blow up the fort," Bonham was with him. Save for his mission out of the Alamo on February 16, the fortress had remained his home.

  Now Travis was infinitely more weary than Bonham. In one of the few times the commander of the Alamo could relax and let his concern be seen, he told his friend what he had decided. This scouting mission had to succeed. All the others must have failed. Fannin surely did not know how many men Santa Anna had in Béxar. Bonham was to impress these facts on Fannin's mind. He must stress two things: that their already overwhelming enemy was receiving reinforcements without halt while the Texans, who needed them, had not received any at all; and that Fannin and the men of Goliad could still get through the Alamo gates. After all, for the past three nights, and once in broad daylight, the Texans had scoured freely the land outside the walls and had not lost a man in the skirmishes. They had set fire to the *jacales* on the south; they had made a diversionary fight on Mexican cavalry to protect the Texas detail sacking houses on the east; they had a third time gone out after dark to clear the north area around the Alamo of any form of cover or protection for the enemy. Fannin could bring his men in if only he had the nerve, if only he realized the urgent need.

It was a moment of tragic irony for the two South Carolinians, and a very bitter one for Travis. Bonham would not have been there at all if Travis had not written him to hurry out to Texas, the "land of the future."

There was nothing more central in Jim Bonham's character than the urge to fight for what he thought was right. He was born with a passionate devotion to justice. He was glad he was there. And he would be back as fast as time and prayer and God's will would allow. They looked at each other, each seeking to strengthen the other's will. Bonham left. Travis called him back.

Bonham would need a signal, he said, for his return. "Tie a white handkerchief around your hat. I'll have men watching from the walls. We'll see you and be ready with the gates."

Silently Travis went up a ramp to a wall-top platform to watch his friend ride away under cover of the brush that grew along the *acequias*. It might be the last time he would see him.

Thus Bonham rode away from the fortress he had come to San Antonio to destroy.

TRAVIS'S STRENGTH was diminished with Bonham gone. He was now transparently stalling for time. He had to spare his men and he had to spare his supplies. He committed one act of desperation. He sent out two more couriers. Doubt was now gnawing at his mind. He remembered how Fannin had wavered about the Matamoros campaign. If Fannin really planned to come, he would surely have reached the Alamo no later than February 28. So, on the night of the twenty-ninth Travis sent out two of the ten Mexicans who had cast their lot with the Texans.

This time, Travis did not choose his couriers. He called for volunteers. There were none. This could mean that the men now regarded courier service as a death trap from which there was no return; or it could mean they thought to volunteer for the service was a craven way of escaping from the fort. Travis decided to draw lots; the die fell on Captain Juan Seguin. Now it was Travis's turn to refuse; he did not want to lose Seguin from his command in the Alamo, in case the courier did not make it back. Seguin gave Travis much support, and the possible need for his knowledge of Spanish and of the people of San Antonio was obvious. The men grumbled at the indecision. Get it over and be done with it. Was not Seguin's knowledge of Spanish at this moment the best asset for a messenger?

Nobody could doubt Seguin's loyalty and competence. His father, Don Erasmo Seguin, was one of the most distinguished citizens of Coahuila y Texas, as well as one of the wealthiest. Don Erasmo owned a famous ranch just below San Antonio, where he had built a pleasant *hacienda*, made out of red sandstone walls but nonetheless called "Casa Blanca." His herds of horses and cattle were vast; the Seguin family had been thriving ever since the first ancestor came with the Canary Island settlers. Don Erasmo, as well as his son, had early chosen to oppose Santa Anna. The father had been one of a two-man welcoming committee, along with Juan de Veramendi, personally nominated by Governor Martinez, to go to Natchitoches to greet Stephen F. Austin upon his first arrival with new colonists. Austin and Don Erasmo had greatly esteemed each other. It was Don Erasmo who had served as Texas deputy to the National Congress at Mexico City when the democratic Constitution of 1824 had been formulated.

Ten years later, on November 15, 1834, Erasmo Seguin had issued a call for a constitutional convention of Texans at San Antonio de Béxar to protest Santa Anna's tyranny. His note had gone unheeded, but he had not wavered in his principles. He helped make the "1824" flag which the Texans unfurled at the Alamo. Over the years the Seguins had proved their steadfastness.

Yet Travis had agreed with Governor Henry Smith that "you could never trust a Mexican." Travis trusted Captain Juan Seguin now.

He instructed Seguin and one of his aides, Antonio Cruz y Arocha, to ride for Gonzales to organize help there, then on to the provisional government to demand relief. Perhaps Travis feared that Jim Bonham had not got through after all. Seguin and his aide, speaking Spanish, might pass unnoticed as citizens of San Antonio. If challenged they could still feign innocence and get away. As horsemen they were expert. Seguin, having no horse in the Alamo *cuartel*, borrowed Jim Bowie's. The Mexican was not sure, he reported later, that Bowie in his fever was really aware he was lending his horse to an old friend.

No courier dispatched since the siege began had come back. The men were almost as eager for news of the world outside as they were for reinforcements.

Seguin and Arocha made their exit late that night, riding toward the east. The night was clear and presently their trail led them by one of the Mexican patrols. The Mexicans, dismounted at the moment, yelled out to the two scouts to halt and approach. Seguin had his plan ready. He called out consent in Spanish and headed toward the camp spot of the Mexican cavalry. This feint having partially reassured the patrol, Seguin and Arocha suddenly spurred their horses, leaned over their sides for protection, and dashed full speed into a thicket. The volley of pistol fire missed them in the confusion; they made their escape and raced toward Gonzales.

Though they had got away, Santa Anna was preparing to undo whatever they might accomplish. He knew of the planned Texas reinforcement from Goliad and dispatched General Ramirez y Sesma that night with a detachment of cavalry and infantry in the same direction. Ramirez was to intercept and annihilate any help from Fannin; his orders did not mention possible reinforcements from any other source. Santa Anna's spy system was working more effectively than Travis's calls for help.

After spending the night on the road, Ramirez reported early next morning from the Mission of San Francisco de la Espada that he had met no enemy nor seen any trace of one. He and his men returned later in the day to camp. Santa Anna, though confident of his numerical superiority, continued to watch the approach from Goliad. He also sent the Battalion of Allende to join the cavalry already posted to the east of the Alamo.

10

In Goliad, the issue had been decided twenty-four hours before Seguin and Arocha set out. It may even have been decided the day that James W. Fannin was born, for the key to the fate of the Alamo garrison lay in the character of the Goliad commander.

Fannin had almost 500 volunteers from the States, mostly from the South, the best-trained and best-equipped army the Texans ever put in the field. Captain Burr H. Duval, writing to his father, then governor of Florida, from Goliad exclaimed: "I have never seen such men as this army is composed of—no man ever thinks of surrender or retreat. They must be exterminated to be whipped. Nothing can depress their ardor. We are frequently for days with nothing but bully beef to eat, and after working hard all day, you could at night hear the boys crowing, gobbling, barking, bellowing, laughing, and singing, you would think them the happiest and best fed men in the world."

Fannin knew what he had and he meant to make it serve his personal glory. Chance had put him where Sam Houston should have been.

James W. Fannin was a magnetic man who charmed people as diverse as New Orleans money lenders, Georgia youths eager to fight for Texas, and even Santa Anna's leading general, José Urrea. When he came to Texas in 1834, he was engaged in disguised slave trading. By Mexican law no slaves were permitted in the territory; Fannin smuggled them in as "free Negroes." The efforts of the Texan settlers meant nothing without sufficient labor; a man's wealth in those days was gauged, not by how many farmlands he had, but by how many servants or slaves. To overcome the Mexican ban on slavery, the Texans had early hit on the solution of calling their Negroes "indentured servants." In this way Fannin came to get rich. A year after his arrival he had formed a partnership with prosperous Joseph Mims of Brazoria in which each invested $25,000. Fannin's contribution consisted of twenty-three "African negroes" worth $17,250 and a note for $7,750.

The partnership was organized on January 12, 1836, just before Fannin, with supreme self-confidence, assumed command of the proposed Texan attack on Matamoros. Fannin had written his friends and supporters in his native Georgia that to take over Texas from the Mexicans might require "a little fighting," but that the rewards would be well worth it. For ten years he had been persuading friends of his money-making gifts, even though his life was a record of unfulfilled promises to pay. His optimism was evidently contagious.

It must be said of James Fannin that he had a warm heart. He was unable to refuse anyone anything. On one slave smuggling trip to Cuba, he bought for his half-sister two parrots, two guinea pigs, two blue-headed ring-striped pigeons, plus a vast collection of sea shells.

It was this boyish, vain, ambitious, impetuous man who became the agent of whatever remnant of government the Texans had in January and February of 1836. Acting Governor Robinson authorized Fannin on February 13 to assume leadership, in essence, of Texas until the Constitutional Convention scheduled for March 1 could form a new government. Robinson wrote the ex-West Pointer: "You will occupy such points as in your opinion you deem best.... Fortify and defend Goliad and Béxar and give the enemy battle if he advances." To make his instructions absolutely clear, Robinson took over Sam Houston's title and signed himself "acting governor and commander in chief of the army." His last sentence constituted a complete handing over of the reins to Fannin: "All former orders given by General Houston or myself are countermanded so you may do as you deem expedient."

Fannin had feuded with Houston over command of the volunteer army; he had carefully kept his command of the Matamoros division separate from the more or less private army of Johnson and Grant. Acting Governor Robinson legitimized his ambition. He was in charge.

By February 13 Fannin had news that plunged him into another extremist attitude, this time of pessimism. He knew for a certainty that Urrea had over a thousand troops at Matamoros and was on the march to Texas. He knew, as all the other Texan leaders did, that Santa Anna had left Saltillo to lead the invasion himself, though he believed, as did the others, that the Mexican general would linger at the Rio Grande. Fannin was completely intimidated by the situation, and acted accordingly. Just as he had left West Point after eighteen months because of a fight, he abandoned the Matamoros project and holed up at fortress Goliad.

His decision made, he put his men to creating of Goliad a toy gem of a fort. What they needed was practice in drill, in sharpshooting, in horseback maneuvering, in frontier warfare. Fannin turned them into day laborers, digging ditches. A sally port was opened onto a covered runway to the river 200 yards from the fort, to insure water supply in case of emergency. Twelve small cannon were placed for effective defense. Crumbling walls were shored up. His smart young captain, John Sowers Brooks, cunningly devised a frontier equivalent of the machine gun, lining up one hundred rifles that could be fired in a chain reaction from one lighted torch. For six weeks, while Houston parleyed with the Cherokees in East Texas and Travis demanded aid from Fannin, these choice troops polished and perfected a fort they would never use.

In the meantime, their commander was having fits of depression. He besought Robinson to make decisions. He doubted his own wisdom, and discovered that he had little gift for commanding men once war became truly imminent. He begged to be relieved of his command, so that he might go and visit his family; then, in his next letter to Robinson, he again struck a vainglorious attitude, wondering whether anybody in Texas, including Houston, was adequate to command an army.

Fannin tried to hide his weakness even from himself. His facile optimism ministered to a deep self-distrust, perhaps stemming from his father's rejection of him as a child. Until he left West Point, which he had entered in 1819 at the age of fourteen, he went by the name of James J. Walker, taking the name of his mother's father, who reared him. Action was a form of escape for him, until action became crucial. Then he dissolved in indecision. Like Travis, he was one of the earliest agitators for total independence. Fannin even wrote a former West Point friend in the U.S. Army, Major Belton, that independence would be declared in 1835 and that Belton should come to take over the Texan army.

It was not possible to be optimistic at Goliad that abnormally cold and dismal winter of 1836. The *presidio* commanded a high rocky elevation on the south side of the San Antonio River, its sister mission several hundred yards to the north. Like the Alamo, the fort at Goliad occupied about three acres, enclosed by a 10-foot-high wall. The fort's chapel had a flat roof which gave sentries a perfect view for miles around. Proud of his work in putting the fort into shape, Fannin called on his men for a new name. He settled on three choices and drew the winner from slips in a hat. "Fort Defiance" won out over the other two: "Independence" and "Milam."

Fort Defiance was well provisioned with food and supplies, but it lacked horses and oxen for transport. Both Johnson and Grant had gone off in mid-January on a scout along the coast for horses, either wild ones they could capture or what they might buy at outlying Mexican *rancherias*.

The fort also lacked discipline, not unusual in the

Texan army. In their instinct for insubordination, the volunteers were only imitating their superiors: Sam Houston had called Fannin away from Béxar the previous November in order to set him up as his chief aide, and yet Fannin had grasped at the chance for greater command in the split between Governor Smith and the Council. Johnson and Grant were openly at odds with Houston about the Matamoros venture; Travis and Bowie were locked in a bitter struggle for command at the Alamo.

From February 9 till March 9, Fannin emptied his supply of rhetoric daily in desperate appeals for help to Acting Governor Robinson and the Advisory Committee of the Council. He wanted above all orders. At the very moment that fate had placed him irrevocably in the position of command, he was turning submissive. He knew it, but he fought its implications. The war was no longer a skylarking preface to riches; it was a matter of admitting that even Texans were vulnerable to thirst and disease and famine and the violent caprices of luck. Fannin continued to implore the Advisory Committee to let him retreat; at the same time he admitted that the responsibility to decide was his, that because of Houston's furlough, he, Fannin, was in charge of the army "naturally and by right."

Travis and Bowie obviously thought this too; they had been sending out appeals to Fannin to send men to the Alamo weeks before Santa Anna arrived. Fannin put off making a decision; it was easier to write another letter to the committee or the acting governor.

And yet some thought him a man of brave heart. Houston esteemed his military capacities; a number of the volunteers serving with him at Goliad admired him greatly. If Sam Houston had not wrecked the Matamoros venture, whose success would have meant alliance with liberal Mexico rather than Houston's wish for an independent republic, Fannin would never have been cast in this central role in resisting Santa Anna. But if the Council had not wrecked Houston's authority, out of hostility to his patron, Governor Smith, Houston would not have abandoned Texan leadership to Fannin in the fatal months of January and February.

It is not surprising that the Texan settlers, confused by such division of command, left the first battles almost entirely to the volunteers from the States. They could hardly feel loyalty to squabbling leaders. Fannin berated them unreasonably: "I have not as much confidence in the people of Texas as I once had. . . . I feel too indignant to say more about them. If I was honorably out of their service, I would never re-enter it. But I must now play a bold game. I will go the whole hog. If I am lost, be the censure on the right head, and may my wife and my children and children's children curse the sluggards forever."

Meanwhile, Fannin's supplies were exhausted, his outposts about to be intercepted by Urrea, his Matamoros venture at a standstill, his decision about the Alamo still unmade. But he was resolute about one thing: he refused to move the chief Texan army under his own initiative. This magnetic man, who had lured dozens of Georgia investors to subsidize his Texas plantation dreams, was himself magnetized by Goliad.

The old fort continued to loom gray above the cedars and white rocks of Goliad. The Indians had abandoned it; the Spaniards had left soon after. Only Fannin seemed rooted to the place.

And like a magnet, it drew couriers from the Alamo

so steadily that John Sowers Brooks said that Fannin heard from Travis almost twice a day.

TRAVIS'S FIRST COURIER to Goliad after Santa Anna's arrival reached Fannin on February 25. Scout Johnson had left the Alamo late in the afternoon of the twenty-third, almost the exact hour Jim Bonham returned. Fannin had already refused to commit himself to Bonham; he was still unwilling when Johnson arrived. Like Houston, Fannin had never thought it wise to regard the Alamo as the gateway to Texas. But now he knew that duty compelled him to try to raise the siege. Issuing the orders for a march, he wrote Acting Governor James W. Robinson: "I am aware that my present move towards Béxar is anything but a military one—the appeals of Cols. Travis and Bowie cannot however pass unnoticed. . . . Sanguine, chivalrous volunteers—much must be risked to relieve the besieged. . . ."

The mercurial Fannin told his aide, Captain Brooks, to prepare for an early morning departure on the twenty-sixth. He would leave 100 men at the garrison, take 400 along with four pieces of artillery, two six-pounders and two fours.

Two days late, the rescue troops finally left Goliad on the morning of the twenty-eighth, the men inadequately clothed, many of them without shoes, and with very little ammunition and very little provender. All his baggage wagons and artillery were drawn by oxen, since no broken horses were at hand.

From the first there was trouble. As they were crossing the San Antonio river only a few hundred yards beyond the fort, three of the wagons broke down. At great hazard the soldiers saved the four cannon and finally, after getting into the water themselves, got them across. The ammunition wagon remained on the other side of the river —presumably to keep the powder dry—while the troops made camp that night on the spot.

The exhausted oxen meanwhile had no fodder. Turned loose to graze on roots and stubble, they wandered during the night. The next morning they could not be found. While each man had twelve rounds of cartridges, the major ammunition and food supplies were on the opposite bank of the river. There were no animals to haul them.

Fannin called a council of war. Action was obviously necessary, but before a decision could be made five fugitives came riding up frantically. One was Colonel Francis Johnson, who had escaped with the four others from capture by Colonel Urrea, leading Santa Anna's other force up the coast, at San Patricio, only fifty miles away. The rest of Johnson's men had been captured or killed. Goliad was now threatened by the enemy.

In the bushes on the banks of the San Antonio river, Fannin's council decided there was only one thing to do: go back. With the same puffing and groaning as before, but with men now doing the work of the oxen, they returned to the fortress Goliad. They had already written off the Alamo in their minds. . . .

TRAVIS NEED NOT have worried about his other couriers. They got through. Dr. Sutherland and John W. Smith, halting frequently because of Sutherland's lame knee, reached Gonzales shortly after dark on the twenty-fourth, a ride of seventy miles in thirty hours.

The town of Gonzales was pleasantly lo-
cated near the junction of the two prettiest streams in
Texas, the San Marcos and the Guadalupe. The Indians had
burned down the first Anglo-American town established
there, in 1825. The colonists, who had come in with *empresario* Green DeWitt in the most successful colonizing
effort after Stephen F. Austin's, returned in 1827. Because
it was the hub, so to speak, between the American colonies
to its east and the "Spanish country" of San Antonio
directly to its west, Gonzales was a central clearinghouse
for news of all Texas. It was here, in what is often called
"the first battle in the Texan Revolution," that the settlers
had refused to give up the cannon requested by Colonel
Ugartechea of the Mexican occupational army. It was here,
when Ugartechea insisted the cannon was a loan (which

it was) and not a gift (as the Texans maintained), that
Albert Martin and the other Gonzales men had draped the
sign over the cannon with its invitation to come and take
it, an invitation which the Mexican squad declined. From
the eighteen men available to fight in Gonzales on September 30, the volunteers grew to 160 by October 2. Travis,
quite naturally, thought the Alamo would get the same
rush of help. The men of Gonzales were determined not to
let him down, to behave as before. Despite the fighting, the
Texans still had not up to March 2—the ninth day of the
Alamo siege—declared either war or independence. Even
if the convention, which met on March 1, had done so, the
men at the Alamo had no way of knowing it.

At Gonzales the reinforcements were assembling.
When Smith and Sutherland came through on the twenty-
fourth, the Gonzales volunteers sent couriers into other
townships and settlements but decided to wait for Fannin's
expedition in order to provide maximum surprise. By the
twenty-ninth it became clear in Gonzales that Fannin was
not coming. Unable to ride in with the regular army, the
thirty-two men from Gonzales who had been ready for
days hastened on their way alone. Their swelling of the
Alamo numbers could mean little in the final outcome, and
this they knew.

Theirs was a decision to die. These men, unlike those
in the Alamo, had all the latest news of the colonies. They
knew that without Fannin's help no other Texas army
could be readied in time to save the Texans besieged at the
Béxar fortress. They knew that Santa Anna had to be delayed in San Antonio as long as possible to let the Texans
form a government and a new army. They knew that their

home town of Gonzales would be next to be swallowed up. But they also knew with unmistakable clarity that they had a duty to the men in the Alamo. When one of the youths asked how they were going to get back, Albert Martin, himself only recently arrived from the Alamo, reportedly said, "Hell, man, we haven't got in yet. Let's go!" Certain of death, either on the road or in the fortress, they set out on February 29 and were on the outskirts of Béxar by dusk of the next day. Their leaders, Captains George C. Kimball and Albert Martin, turned over leadership to Scout John W. Smith who was to guide them through the Mexican lines and the Texan outposts.

The thirty-two men from Gonzales carried with them the first flag ever made by the Texans for battle use. It was made of white silk, from the wedding dress of Naomi DeWitt, who had married W. A. Matthews at Gonzales in 1833. Her mother was the leading spirit in Gonzales, taking over after the death in 1835 of her husband, Green DeWitt. When Colonel Ugartechea's men came to her with his demand for the cannon, she alerted Albert Martin and then made a war flag from her daughter's wedding dress. The words "Come and Take It" appeared twice on it—above and below the black cannon in the flag's center. The men from Gonzales now carried it with them toward the Alamo.

Smith led the approach to the fortress with the greatest caution. The entrance was to be maneuvered after midnight, when fires would be low and attention relaxed. Once beyond the Mexican patrols, there was the danger of being mistaken by the Texan sentries for enemy. When Smith gave the signal, the little troop made its way silently and under cover of brush along the irrigation ditches. They suffered only one casualty, and that one slight. It did not even come from Mexican fire. Before he recognized them or heard the password, an Alamo sentry fired once and hit one of the Gonzales men in the foot.

The shot was a prelude to wild noise inside the walls. The news spread through the Alamo that help had come. It was almost three in the morning, but every man now rushing to the gates was awake and buoyant with hope. As sleep fell from their eyes, they shouted their relief. For a moment there was consternation when the size of the support became known. Only thirty-two! Why, that still made a total inside the fort of less than 200 men. But hope was reborn at the sight of men capable of such sacrifice and courage.

They reassured each other and privately thought, "We'll live now." If thirty-two came through this night, surely hundreds would follow—tomorrow. Sleep was of no use now. This was a chance to celebrate and they needed desperately some cause for new hope. The low-burning camp fires were piled high with wood, freshly slaughtered beef was brought, and the Alamo garrison entertained its new guests regally. There was more to eat than usual but it was more of the same thing. Beef and corn. Corn and beef. But in that dawn they ate of eternity and salvation.

THE STREAM of relief from the colonies seemed at long last to be flowing. That night, the men from Gonzales spared them the truth.

Dr. Amos Pollard, Captain Almeron Dickinson, and six other men from Gonzales led the welcoming celebration. Of all Texas cities, little Gonzales had furnished the Alamo with its fullest roster. With the new arrivals, there were now forty of its citizens in the garrison, including Mrs. Dickinson and her baby.

Dr. Pollard answered the newcomers' questions about Jim Bowie. He was a sick man, indeed, but still full of fight. Just that noon Bowie had had one of his good moments. He insisted on being carried down into the court to speak a while with the men. He entreated them to recognize the valor of Travis and to give him their loyalty. He promised to hound them in hell if they didn't. As his spirits strengthened, he got another inspired idea. He would show the men that he and Travis had fully resolved all past difficulties and had forgotten them.

"Bill," he called. Bowie had a request. He explained that in his less fevered moments he had done a deal of studying of enemy movements. There was a steady ebb and flow of enemy brass to the southwest where the Ramon Músquiz house faced the Antonio de la Garza dwelling. Santa Anna was bound to be in headquarters there, in the house where Susanna Dickinson had waited for her husband eight days ago. Two balls fired from the twelve-pounder at the platform on the southwest angle might blow Santa Anna and his staff halfway to hell. Travis nodded in agreement. He needed to hoard that shot, but he ordered the discharge. The men scrambled to where they could see, ducking the Mexican rifle fire. "Fire in the hole!" yelled the cannoneer, and the Texans stood clear. A great blast hit the Músquiz walls squarely and exploded stones into the air. The second ball broke right on target.

At the same moment, a Texan at watch on the walls yelled, "There he is!" And they saw the gleaming elegance of General Santa Anna, but not as they hoped. The *Caudillo* had crossed the bridge and was personally inspecting Mexican preparations. The damage to his headquarters in the Músquiz house had left him unscathed.

Texas rifles quickly drew a bead on the general. Thus far, these guns, rather than the light artillery, had kept the Mexican lines at a distance. It may have been this that saved the general. He was too far away for their rifles. But he made an undignified dash for cover and gave the Texans their heartiest laugh to date. Colonel Almonte recorded that his superior was angry the rest of the day.

Even so, Santa Anna's inspection of how far his commands had been executed should have pleased him. By March 1, he had the Alamo encircled, with strong batteries from nearly all points trained on the fort. His entrenchments had daily moved in closer and closer. The investment of the siege was almost complete, with escape cut off on the east and with approach of reinforcement almost certain of swift detection. Some, including Dr. Sutherland, even believed that he let the Gonzales band of thirty-two men get through deliberately in order to swell the kill.

Santa Anna was still firing his light artillery pieces from half a mile away. Damage to fortress walls had been very slight, with no breach yet opened. Before any final assault he would have to get his cannon closer. Colonel Ampudia had the soldiers digging trenches closer under the cover of darkness each night. The Alamo could not expect the big push to be postponed much longer. The Mexican numbers were swelling with the almost daily arrival of new columns. The cannon, though not of true siege caliber, were growing in number too. By the eighth day of the siege, a dozen batteries were trained on the fort, some a thousand yards away, others as near as 300 yards. The cavalry on the east had been joined by infantry to cut down fugitives and intercept any harassment of their flanks from other Texas forces.

This was the prospect that greeted the thirty-two men from Gonzales as dawn broke on the morning of March 2. They could see plainly what they had only suspected when they had come in last night under cover of dark. They were trapped, the Alamo was menaced from every direction. Now they too, like Travis and the other men at the Alamo, gave thought to Jim Bonham's mission, to Captain Juan Seguin and his search for aid.

Many of the new men knew Jim Bonham, and their hope lived on the faith they put in him. They could not have had a better spokesman. Bonham was not just a great scout, an unflagging and indefatigable horseman, but a born leader, a persuasive lawyer. If any man could persuade Fannin to change his mind, Bonham could.

All that day, the Mexican bombardment increased in volume. Somebody, perhaps, had caught the whiplash of the general's wrath for letting the reinforcements through. General Santa Anna ordered an intensive search for trails that might ease couriers in or out of the fort. In the afternoon he found one, just within pistol shot of the Alamo. How it went undiscovered so long is puzzling. At any rate, Santa Anna further tightened the vise by ordering the battalion of Ximenes to guard the roadway.

The Texans, and particularly the men from Gonzales, saw this order executed from their walls. It filled them with a wordless melancholy. With all the pathways sealed, how could even one courier, riding in alone, find a way into the Alamo?

Still, Travis did not entirely share this gloom. With Jim Bonham still to be heard from, he would keep hoping. Bonham had been gone five days. He was due back. Every pair of eyes in the Alamo watched the east. They could not live without Bonham. But they heard no hoofbeats on the stony roads between the blasts of the twelve Mexican batteries.

What hope for reinforcements remained vanished entirely on Thursday, March 3. Travis learned the bitter and inescapable truth when, at eleven o'clock that morning, Bonham returned from his mission of February 27.

Bonham returned to the outskirts of San Antonio with one other courier, possibly two. When the riders halted to get the lay of the land, Bonham's companion thought the Mexican army now had closed in too tightly to allow anyone to get back in the Alamo. Bonham alone decided to try. He thought Travis was entitled to the news which Fannin, after turning back on February 28, had not troubled to send.

Bonham dashed through the picket south gate, his

169

white horse now dark with sweat. Tied to his hat in the prearranged signal of identity was a white handkerchief. The startled Mexicans—momentarily inert at so daring a midmorning ride through their lines—grabbed their guns and opened brisk fire. Bonham leaned his six-foot-two frame over the side of his mount, and hanging low, rode through the open gate unscathed. Travis's last letter written that same day merely says that Bonham reentered the garrison unmolested. What harm to Santa Anna if another gringo rode back into his trap? Any and all were welcome. More fuel for the funeral fire.

Fannin had shared his grim view and had advised Bonham not to return, that to go back into the Alamo was suicidal. "I will make my report to Travis," Bonham answered him, "or die in the attempt."

The only triumphant thing about Bonham's return was his safe entrance into the fort. His news was simple and sad: Fannin would not come. The irresolute, West Point-trained commander of the main Texas army at Goliad had delayed too long. Bonham told Travis of Fannin's half-hearted start and the decision of the council to turn back and make Goliad invincible. For Travis this could mean but one thing. Fannin and the men at Goliad thought the Alamo had no chance of survival, with or without reinforcements.

For Travis it was the supreme blow. It was more than that. To Travis's mind, it all seemed predestined, the web of fatality.

Most of Travis's life had been shadowed by tragedy. There was the uncertainty about his parentage, an improbable story that Travis Senior had found him in a basket. There was his unhappy marriage and the uncertainty about his wife's fidelity. There was his undeserved fifty-day imprisonment at Anáhuac, and his return three years later to drive away the tariff-collector, for which premature action he had been bitterly denounced by Austin's colonists and the Texas Peace Party. He had had to print a card asking the colonists to delay judgment till time revealed the reality of things. A girl at San Felipe keeping a diary recorded that "It was hot-headed William Barret Travis who precipitated the war with Santa Anna."

He was not hotheaded now. He was a leader of men who trusted him, who had believed with him that the Alamo stand was sensible because relief was in sight. Now he—they—had been abandoned. The commander in chief of the Texas army turned all his attention to political problems. Fannin still at Goliad. Houston meeting with the Council at Washington-on-the-Brazos. The farmers tending their flocks, caring for their families. Only Travis and his handful of men at the Alamo.

If Travis was indignant now, it was not at fate, but at all the slow-moving prudent people of this world, the cool-minded Austins and Houstons, the gradualists and the complex, at all minds which calculate possibilities and weigh one side against the other. For Travis there was never but one side.

THE DAY WAS as happy for the Mexicans as it was depressing for Travis and the Texans. General Santa Anna recessed his honeymoon to admire the placing of the new battery right under the Texans' noses. The success of this maneuver was more exhilarating than the arrival during the afternoon of the *zapadores*, or sappers, of Aldama and

Tolucca. Now the Mexican army at San Antonio de Béxar was probably 5,000 strong.

The Mexican welcome to the Tolucca *zapadores* and to those of Aldama, comprising probably an additional 1,500 men, was thunderous. Parades enlivened the main plaza, the bands played raucously and the bells of San Fernando Church clanged in the air—the same bells young Cloud had rung ten days ago to announce the arrival of Santa Anna's troops.

These reinforcements were not the only cause for this jubilation. A dispatch had arrived from the eastern command of the Mexican army, the detachment under General Urrea, informing the Mexicans of what Colonel Fannin had already learned—that in sweeping up the coast to head off the portion of the Texas army infected with Matamoros fever, Urrea had made contact with an outer flank of the Texas force near San Patricio, twenty miles from the coast. The triumphant message from Urrea stated that he had routed the revolutionaries, killing sixteen and taking twenty-one prisoners. Santa Anna was only partially pleased; he sternly reminded Urrea of his instructions: that in this war there were to be no prisoners. To the Mexican troops, however, this first real shooting encounter with the rebels became an omen, a favorable augury for the whole campaign.

Inside the Alamo, where every peal of the bells shook the Texans' hearts, surmise alone could interpret the celebration. Travis guessed that only one thing—short of his own defeat—could provoke such cavorting. General Santa Anna must not have been in the town all these days but must only have just arrived. But it was not Santa Anna who was being feted. It was the welcome news to the ordinary

Mexican soldier that Texans could be defeated. After ten days of besieging the Alamo, many of Santa Anna's soldiers had begun to wonder whether the Texans could be conquered at all—even with 1,500 more comrades at arms from Aldama and Tolucca. But now Urrea had done it.

From their platforms by the walls the Texans could see the Plaza fanfare. No wonder they thought the Mexican army must be 10,000 strong: the locust swarm in the square looked as though a retaining dike against the pressure of humanity had burst. People flooded the space before the church and there were thousands, it seemed, of women. The Mexican soldier traveled with his *mujer*, his *soldadera* and his offspring, and even the camp followers had followed their men across the desert to cook and minister to their comforts. The officers of the army delighted in this colorful auxiliary. It reminded them of their military life in Europe. Hungry for women, the watching Texans had their own thoughts.

The commotion below seemed to clear Travis's mind. There were letters to send now or never. With new Mexican reinforcements continually arriving, couriers would hardly be able to get through. It was only yesterday that Santa Anna had discovered the concealed dirt road. Plainly he wanted the exit of no more scouts. As for the roads down which reinforcements might come, he was not worried. His spies kept him posted. He knew of Fannin's departure from Goliad and of his swift turning back. General Ramirez's report had assured him that no enemy troops were on their way. Santa Anna knew, then, two days before Travis, that the men in the Alamo had no hope of relief from Fannin. Sam Houston was their final prospect.

Travis, at his table in the dark room, pulled a candle

near him and began to write. Perhaps a scout as expert as John W. Smith could make one more *sortie*. Even if he did not get through—and to do so he would have to crawl after dark on his hands and knees down the irrigation canal—the final appeal to Governor Henry Smith and Commander-in-chief Sam Houston had to be made. Uncertain as to what action the convention had taken, Travis addressed his message simply to the president of the group, whoever the new man might be.

Travis began: "In the present confusion of the political authorities of the country, and in the absence of the commander-in-chief, I beg leave to communicate to you the situation of this garrison." A summary of enemy activities from February 25 to March 3 follows. "The enemy," he continues, "have kept up a bombardment from two howitzers, one a five and a half inch, the other an eight inch, and a heavy cannonade from two long nine-pounders, mounted on a battery on the opposite side of the river, at a distance of four hundred yards from our wall. During this period the enemy have been busily employed in encircling us with entrenched encampments on all sides. . . .

"I have fortified this place, so that the walls are generally proof against cannon balls; and I shall continue to entrench on the inside, and strengthen the walls by throwing up dirt. At least two hundred shells have fallen inside of our works without having injured a single man; indeed, we have been so fortunate as not to lose a man from any cause, and we have killed many of the enemy. The spirits of the men are still high though they have had much to depress them."

Travis says enemy strength has been estimated variously, from 1,500 to 6,000 men. At least a thousand are entering Béxar from the west as he writes. By the time he gets to a postscript, he has altered this figure: "The enemy's troops are still arriving, and the reinforcements will probably number two or three thousand."

He has given up hope of aid from Fannin. "I have *repeatedly* sent to him for aid without receiving any." So now, he can look "to the colonies alone for aid; unless it arrives soon, I shall have to fight the enemy on his own terms." He notes the garrison has provisions for another twenty days but that they need ammunition desperately.

Again he justifies the decision to stay and defend the Alamo: "The power of Santa Anna is to be met here or in the colonies; we had better meet them here than to suffer a war of devastation to rage in our settlements."

A blood-red flag was waving, he says, not only in the church but in the "camp above us." These threats of "no quarter" have only strengthened the "high souled courage" of his men.

Once again Travis gives vent to his dislike of Mexicans. His letter is particularly bitter against the citizens of San Antonio:

> The citizens of this municipality are all our enemies, except those who have joined us heretofore. We have three Mexicans now in the fort [Travis had sent others out on scouting missions]; those who have not joined with us in this extremity, should be declared public enemies, and their property should aid in paying the expenses of the war.

Thus, quite unfairly, Travis transferred his anger at the Texas colonists, who had not joined up either, to his Mexican neighbors. Certainly the predicament of the hapless

Mexican citizens of Béxar—forced to choose between possible Mexican reprisals and Texas independence—was tormenting. Their homes were much closer to the menace than those of the Anglo settlers in colonies hundreds of miles away. It would have been against nature for them to imagine that 180 or so Texans could possibly defeat the thousands of Santa Anna's soldiers they saw daily in the streets. Their neutrality, under the circumstances, was understandable.

Travis' conclusion to his letter is his rubric: "God and Texas—Victory or Death."

The tone in this last letter Travis dispatched to Governor Smith or his successor has a new resonance and depth lacking perhaps in his famous first appeal. It is as heroic as before but now with the mellowness of a man who has discovered his own humanity in the suffering of brave men around him. He is calm when he reports that he knows the Texas division into a civil war of politics still prevails, despite the unifying force of an enemy presence on Texas soil. He does not berate anyone for this. Instead, he calmly makes a battle report, with the needful details. His mind is operating with great clarity as a battle commander and not as a crusader.

Again without berating Fannin, he writes off that hope and makes this last appeal to the Convention itself. But the heart of the message is his tribute of confidence to "my men": "The determined valor and the desperate courage, heretofore exhibited by my men, will not fail them in the last struggle."

The phrase has the ring of finality. Now Travis knew that the boys who had come from far away, nineteen of them from European countries, were to die almost before they had lived in the landscape of dry air and cactus and mesquite under whose spell they had fallen. He had more thought for them than for himself. And a final thought for his courier: "The bearer of this will give your honorable body a statement more in detail, should he escape through enemy lines."

The bearer, John W. Smith, did make it through the enemy lines. As he set out, shortly after midnight, Travis told him: "Every morning at daybreak, I will fire a cannon as a sign that we still hold the fort, but when the cannon is heard no more, its silence will tell that the Alamo has fallen."

Smith was an excellent scout, and the men were confident that he would make it. He carried many a personal message from the soldiers in the Alamo along with the official papers. Travis himself enclosed several letters, among them one to his friend Jesse Grimes and another, on a torn scrap of wrapping paper, for Rebecca Cummins. He did not write to his wife.

The letter to Grimes illustrates one of the historical ironies which grew out of the confused situation in Texas. The day before Travis wrote, on March 2, the Convention had unanimously adopted the Declaration of Independence. Nobody was pretending any longer to defend the Mexican Constitution of 1824. But the men in the Alamo never knew they were fighting for the Republic of Texas instead of this Mexican constitution. They never heard of their government's action. They had already declared independence for Texas, anyway. As Travis wrote Grimes: "Let the Convention go on and make a declaration of independence, and we will then understand, and the world will understand, what we are fighting for. If independence is not declared,

I shall lay down my arms, and so will the men under my command. But under the flag of independence we are ready to peril our lives a hundred times a day...."

All Travis's last letters were written in this heroic tone, but the one he wrote in regard to his son has a special quality.

Travis was devoted to the seven-year-old boy and had stopped the previous January to pay him a visit and arrange for the boy's keep on his way to his new duties at the Alamo. The youngster was going to school at Montville, the home of David Ayers, where Miss Lydia Anne McHenry maintained a school for young people of the community. The latter's niece, a classmate of Charles, recalled that Colonel Travis was reading at one moment during his visit when son Charles went up to him, drew his head down, and whispered something into his ear.

Colonel Travis smiled, and asked out loud, "My son, what do you want with four bits?"

The boy answered, "I want to buy a bottle of molasses from Mrs. Scott to make some candy."

Travis reached into his pocket. In his eagerness, the boy dropped the money but quickly recovered it before it rolled away. Charles bought the molasses, persuaded the cook to make the candy, and, as Miss McHenry's niece adds, "He divided it among all the rest of us children."

Now, on March 3, in the midst of battle, Travis scribbled two sentences for his son. They were addressed to Jesse Grimes: "Take care of my little boy. If the country should be saved, I may make him a splendid fortune; but if the country should be lost, and I should perish, he will have nothing but the proud recollection that he is the son of a man who died for his country."

The cannons must have been booming; Travis's attention must have been required elsewhere. His note for his son, Charles, survives: a hasty scribbling on a ragged piece of yellow paper.

Later that day he thought of another child, the young daughter of Almeron and Susanna Dickinson. Travis wore a hammered gold ring, set with a black cat's-eye stone, large as a chinaberry. Perhaps with a thought for his own small daughter, a memory that for more than one reason would have plagued him, Travis took this handsome ring off his finger, found a piece of string to run through it, and went to find little Angelina Dickinson. He tied the improvised necklace around her neck. "I won't have any more use for this," he told her, "keep it for me."

THE LAST MAN to leave the Alamo was John W. Smith at midnight on March 3rd; the last to enter was Bonham, for whom the gates had been thrown open at eleven that morning.

There is another story, however, that says another man left after Smith—a former friend of Bowie's and veteran of Napoleon's Moscow campaign, a Frenchman named Louis (Moses) Rose. Of all the incomplete and unproved stories about the Alamo this is the most dramatic and most plausible.

The story of Louis Moses Rose and his escape from the Alamo was first published in 1873, thirty-seven years after the fall, in the *Texas Almanac.* There is evidence that it had oral circulation before that. Whether one is to believe it depends upon one's willingness to listen to a single voice giving evidence no one else can verify. The

W. P. Zuber family of Nacogdoches, who befriended Rose, believed it. They saw the shirts in his bundle still glued together with dried blood. R. B. Blake, Jr., who made the most painstaking study of the story, believed it. He felt that he had proof that a Moses Rose did live in Nacogdoches before and after the fall of the Alamo; that he was in the Alamo before March 3, 1836; and that he did escape, as he claimed, soon after dark on the evening of March 3. Following is the story as Rose told it.

Rose owed his life, he said, to a special speech and gesture which Travis made toward sundown of March 3. Rose had fought beside his close friend, Bowie, all during the campaigns of the past December. At his home, in Nacogodoches, he was paymaster and assistant boss for a trader in cotton and other goods. Moses Rose had been an early immigrant to Texas in 1827, having followed many of his comrades in Napoleon's army when after Waterloo they left the Old World to seek a better fate in the new. He knew Spanish as well as his native French. He had stayed on in San Antonio after the defeat of General Cós, going into the Alamo as one of Jim Bowie's men. He had been there during nine days of siege, been there that morning when Jim Bonham returned from his mission to Fannin.

The Alamo, Rose said, had been incessantly bombarded during the last five days and nights. But on March 3, the Mexicans quit firing two hours before dusk. Silence was where sound had been. It was then that Travis assembled his men and made his last speech.

According to Rose, Travis was overwhelmed by emotion. He had not yet told his men what he had known

since eleven o'clock that morning, that Bonham's mission
had failed, that reinforcements would not come. Now he
paraded all his effective men in single file while Bowie was
brought in on his cot. Travis took his position at the center
in front of the line of men. He was unable to speak for a
few moments. Then he mastered his emotion and began to
describe their common plight.

He first blamed himself. "I have deceived you," Rose
quotes him as saying, "by the promise of help." He had
been deceived, he said, by others. Every letter from the
Texas Council, every report brought in to the Alamo before the siege, had assured Travis and Bowie that the colonies would organize recruits and come to their aid. Travis
had believed that he would have a large enough army to
repel an enemy of any size and to enforce the Texans' own
conditions of surrender and guarantee of peace. And now,
today, it was clear that the promised help had not arrived,
would never arrive in time.

Travis's announcement was met by the silence of his
men. Choosing his words carefully, he continued. The
men must be prepared for the worst. He could no longer
offer hope, either of help or survival. "Our fate is sealed.
Within a very few days—perhaps a very few hours—we
must all be in eternity. This is our destiny and we cannot
avoid it. This is our certain doom."

After excusing the Texas government (surprised like
those in the Alamo by Santa Anna's early arrival) and
Fannin (who, he charitably assumed, might be fighting
Mexicans elsewhere), Travis apologized for having misled
the men. He now proposed to make the situation clear.
Surrender was unthinkable, worse than death; to cut their

way through the enemy lines was impossible. "All that remains is to die in the fort and fight to the last moment. . . . We must sell our lives as dearly as possible."

But every man had his choice. Travis's choice was to fight to the death, "as long as there is breath in my body." After assuring his men that they would be cherished in memory and that their death would give the colonies the spur to save themselves, he concluded with a final sentence and a memorable gesture.

Colonel Travis drew the sword he always carried. In front of the watchful, expectant men, he traced with it a long line over the ground, extending from the right to the left end of the file.

While the men were wondering what the line meant, Travis returned to his place in the center of the column. Studying the faces before him, he said, "I now want every man who is determined to stay here and die with me to come across this line. Who will be the first? March!"

It would be impossible to say what thoughts were in the minds of his men at this moment. Perhaps all their hopes, all they intended to do in life, rose before them. Travis had asked, not for their loyalty, but for their lives. He had asked them to stay and die with him.

Tapley Holland was the first man to cross Travis's line. He leaped eagerly, proud of being first. Others followed—Daniel Cloud, Micajah Autry, Davy Crockett— as fast as they could leap across. It was as though they had left life itself on the other side. At the end, only two were left where a moment before 183 had stood.

Colonel Jim Bowie, unable to rise from his bed, called for help. "Boys," he said, "I am not able to go to you, but

I wish some of you would be so kind as to remove my cot over there." Instantly four men ran to the corners of his cot and lifted him over. There was the noise of cheers.

One man remained. Louis Moses Rose, who had endured the retreat from Moscow, stood staring at the line. Travis had said there was a choice. One could die in the fort, or surrender, or try to escape.

Rose was twice the age of most of the men on the other side of Travis's line. He had already suffered his share of the human burden in the Napoleonic Wars. He had come to the New World to live, not to save it. Now, looking at the dedicated faces of the men on the other side, he knew he did not belong there. With his command of the Mexican speech, there was a chance he might make it. Once out of the fort, he could pass for a Mexican, a citizen of San Antonio, and get away.

His eyes could not leave Jim Bowie. On the other side of the line all eyes were trained on him. His agony of indecision was broken when Bowie spoke to him.

"You seem not to be willing to die with us, Rose!" said Bowie.

"No," Rose replied, "I am not prepared to die, and I shall not do so if I can avoid it."

Davy Crockett spoke up, kindly. "You may as well die with us, old fellow, for you cannot escape."

Rose's eyes measured the height of the wall. Suddenly determined, he seized his bundle of unwashed clothes, sprang forward and climbed to the top. The lull in the firing still held. He looked down for a last moment at his doomed friends, then leaped. He was astonished to see the ground outside covered with slaughtered Mexicans and pools of blood. His bundle opened and several shirts were stained with red. He gathered them up, and fled along the river, making his escape miraculously through the nearly silent town. Cannon fire, beginning again, accompanied him all during the night. Finally, exhausted and gored by thorns and cactus whose wounds he could show till the end of his life, he made his way to East Texas and the porch of the W. P. Zuber family.

The Zubers believed his story—the evidence of the blood-stained shirts seemed incontrovertible—and thirty-seven years later W. P. Zuber, Jr., the son of Rose's old friend, who was away with the Texas army when Rose arrived, wrote the story out. It is on this thirdhand report that the episode of Travis's drawing the line must rest.

The problems in believing the story are—at first sight —many. Young Zuber was not present when Rose arrived. Rose spoke "very broken English." In defending his report, however, Zuber insisted that his mother and father— well aware of the significance of Rose's testimony—made Rose retell his story again and again, until together they had a coherent account. As long as she lived, Mrs. Zuber continued to rehearse the story. When her son decided to write it down to "preserve it for posterity," she, then seventy-eight, carefully reviewed the written version and pronounced it a faithful and accurate report of what she and her husband had carefully preserved in their minds. Zuber does not claim to quote Travis verbatim, but he insists that many phrases are identical with Rose's account and that the general effect is wholly typical of Travis, whom Zuber had known personally. "Probably Rose," R. B. Blake observed, "was peculiarly fitted to carry this speech to the people of Texas, because of the fact that he could not read or write, and had, for that reason, trained his memory to retain what he heard."

There is a psychological factor that tends to strengthen Rose's story. Certainly the episode earns him no credit. He knew that his fellow citizens would regard his escape as cowardly. Rose's private interest was really to suppress what happened. He could easily have lied that he had been dispatched from the fort as a scout. But what Rose did and saw had its own compulsion. Even if it damaged him personally, he had to tell it.

Whatever the facts about the line drawn in dirt by Travis with his sword, one truth towers over all. With Rose gone, the Alamo garrison was now one collective personality. Travis's dedicated courage was the symbol for this unity. The men were now one with each other, individual differences resolved.

Travis was now for these men not merely a forceful, courageous commander. He was a serene individual who gave meaning by his serenity to their decision to die. He was the father and the brother, the image and the mirror, the essence of them all. He had spoken true and this moment of truth bound them forever together.

The last word on Travis and his line belongs to J. Frank Dobie: "I was sixteen or seventeen years old when for the first time I went to San Antonio and entered the Alamo, though I had lived all my life not much over a hundred miles away. As I walked through the low door with my father and mother and came into the darkling light of the ancient fortress—ancient for Texas, and a fortress and not a church for Texans—I looked first for the place where Travis drew the line. . . . Nobody forgets the line. It is drawn too deep and straight."

The poet, Sidney Lanier, visited San Antonio thirty years after the fall of the Alamo. Lanier, threatened by tuberculosis, had come for his health and been greatly stirred by the unique little town with its river meandering, as the Indians said, "like a big drunk," and its atmosphere at once tropical and western.

In his historical study of San Antonio de Béxar, still one of the best ever written, Lanier gives a startling account of Travis's speech. "Let us resolve," he quotes Travis as saying, "to withstand our adversaries to the last, and at each advance to kill as many of them as possible. And when at last they shall storm our fortress, let us kill them as they come! kill them as they scale our wall! kill them as they leap within! kill them as they raise their weapons and as they use them! kill them as they kill our companions! and continue to kill them as long as one of us shall remain alive! ..."

It was, Lanier concludes, "one of the most pathetic days in time."

To the men of the Alamo, however, March 3 was a day, not of despair, but of action. Shortly after the departure of John W. Smith, they began firing at Santa Anna's new battery on the north side. If the skirmish did little to destroy the Mexican position, it accomplished much in strengthening the Texans' morale. They had made their choice and were content with it. They had crossed the line.

AT WASHINGTON-ON-THE-BRAZOS, 140 miles east of the Alamo, March 3 was a day of celebration. At the temporary Texas capital, a party was in progress.

On February 28, delegates for the convention, fortunately scheduled before Governor Smith and the Provisional Council staged their civil war, began to arrive in the miserable little village of some dozen or so log houses, some of them unfinished. The main street was no more than a wagon-rutted trail. Stumps still not uprooted made it difficult going in the best of weather, and now a rain-filled norther had blown into town, dropping the temperature to thirty-three degrees.

Washington, as the Texans called it, was hardly prepared to handle a convention. Once the delegates had struggled through the quagmire to reach the town, they had trouble finding places to stay. Many of them bedded down on their saddle blankets on the damp woodshavings of a carpenter shed. A few had to make shelter under the dripping trees. Arriving on February 29th from his treaty making with the Cherokees, Sam Houston luckily had a warm Indian blanket worn Cherokee-style over his shoulders instead of the Mexican *serape* he usually wore.

It was hard to keep warm during the day. When the convention began its duties on March 1, the delegates had to choose between light to see by and their comfort. They met in a windowless, unfinished frame building, with linen tacked over the openings to bar the merciless cold. Yet they had cause to celebrate. Despite the confusion and the perils of overconfidence, the delegates drew up an impressive declaration of independence, on March 2, and affixed their signatures to it with, appropriately, the quill of an eagle.

Three leading Mexican rebels signed with the Texans. Lorenzo de Zavala was a fugitive from Santa Anna, and a former leader in the Mexican government. He was a true republican and a highly educated man, the most civilized man in Texas, according to William Fairfax Gray. He had represented Mexico abroad as minister to France; he had courageously fought Santa Anna's dissolution of the Mexican republican constitution of 1824. The other two Mexican signers were Don Francisco Ruiz and Don Antonio Navarro, the latter the son of a Corsican who had come to the New World.

But for sickness, they would have been joined by Gaspar Flores and Erasmo Seguin, both of whom had been elected by the department of Béxar as delegates, along with Ruiz, Navarro, Jim Bonham, Jesse Badgett, Sam Maverick, and Amos Pollard. Bonham and Pollard elected to stay with Travis; Seguin was too ill to travel; Flores died on his way to Washington.

The Mexicans signing the declaration now were showing great courage, and the Texans knew it. When the delegates elected David Burnet president of the new government, they named Lorenzo de Zavala vice-president.

The delegates had something else to celebrate besides their declaration. March 2, 1836, was the birthday of Samuel Houston, "Uncle Sam" as the Texans had begun to call him. His presence strengthened their feeling that there would now be no difficulty or delay in joining Texas to the Union. In honor of both events, toddies and grogs accompanied toast upon toast. The delegates were still celebrating on March 3, the day that Travis in the Alamo was drawing his line.

The first of Travis's messages had reached Washington-on-the-Brazos February 29, leap-year day, the day Sam Houston had arrived. The plea had generated alarm and fervor. Governor Smith sent it on to all the towns, with an impassioned entreaty of his own. Then the delegates settled down to their duties. Travis's second courier arrived on March 3. His message contained praise of Despallier and Brown and his gratitude for the counsels of Davy Crockett. But it also spoke out bugle-clear his demand for immediate help. The urgency of his plea could not be denied.

Delegate Robert Potter took the floor and impetuously called on all his colleagues to rush to their horses and speed at once for the Alamo. A dozen men leaped to their feet with cheers. Sam Houston let the storm beat about him for a while, and then his calm imposed itself.

We are no more than the pirates Santa Anna has decreed us, he told the Texans, as long as we do not have an elected government and a declaration of war and independence. He reviewed the situation rapidly but thoughtfully. Their chief asset was time, their chief need money and support and men from the United States. The only strategy was to bring their chaos into a semblance of unity. Otherwise, they could anticipate no real help from north of the border: the risks for American capital were too great. In this most difficult of decisions Houston persuaded them to sit down and function as constitution makers, not as heroes.

It was the hardest decision of Sam Houston's life. He had to choose, not between good and evil, but between two heavy responsibilities.

He knew the Texans could not survive without unity. It was their own civil war, their lack of a political structure, which had permitted the present crisis. He had to choose now between the future survival for all Texas and the immediate plight of the small band at the Alamo. Like many another general, he had to declare men he loved expendable. He made the choice history has judged best.

In this the delegates could only follow him. Houston, to them, was still an enigma. No one really knew what kind of backing he had from President Jackson, if any. No one knew whether General Gaines of the United States Army stationed in Louisiana had moved soldiers near the Texas border in order simply to find a pretext for entering the Texas struggle. The delegates could only put their faith in Houston.

Later, Mrs. Mary Austin Holley, Stephen F. Austin's cousin, berated Houston for his decision. Why, she asked him, did he not hurry to the aid of Travis and Fannin? Houston replied: "The provisional government was in disorder—we had no constitution. Travis was sending for assistance—had none to give—had to make a constitution—no better than pirates without one. *Signed the constitution on my birthday and had a great spree on egg nog that lasted two days!*"

"What!" exclaimed Mrs. Holley, a minister's widow. "With so much at stake, with such a responsibility, could you give yourself so low a pleasure?"

"It was a bad business," admitted Houston. "I hated it, and repented of it."

13

A bleak, bitter norther blew up at midafternoon on March 5. By nightfall the winds had chilled bodies through the marrow of the bones and frozen the crust of the earth. The raging weather hushed for a time the crack of guns, the spit and roar of cannonade. Where blood had spilled on the earth, it hardened in a hurry.

At the end of this twelfth day of the siege, the Texans were still hoarding their powder against the inevitable final assault. The supply they had at the start was "little more than coal dust," almost worthless for rifles and not much better for cannon fire. It was mostly Mexican ammunition captured from General Cós the previous December. This same General Cós was now outside the walls of the fortress he had once commanded, seeking a chance to rehabilitate his reputation. Santa Anna had just decided at

191

two o'clock that Saturday afternoon to give his brother-in-law the place of honor in leading the attack. Against the advice of his better generals, he had decided to storm the Alamo's walls that night. The most exposed and dangerous of the four simultaneous assaults fell to Cós's command—Cós, who had betrayed his pledge never to return to Texas.

Santa Anna meant to give Cós ample opportunity to redeem himself, to erase the humiliation of that surrender.

The Texans held their gunfire because they were short of ammunition, but Santa Anna had silenced the Mexican guns late in the afternoon of the overcast and freezing March day for a different reason. He was always well informed about the strength and supplies of the Texans in the mission-fortress. He knew that his constant cannonade, especially during the long nights, and the real or feigned skirmishes had exhausted Texan nerves as well as ammunition. Now he wanted to give them a chance to sleep the sleep of exhaustion—and awake to find Mexicans scaling the walls.

Up until this sudden cease-fire the Texans had not suffered a single casualty. It was this fact, reported by Travis in his last message on March 3, that now made the threat of loss more terrible. The hand of doom had been stayed for twelve days. How long before it fell—and how heavily?

Travis had watched helplessly the ebb of spirits in his men as the Mexican night sorties and cannonade had wrecked their nerves and sleep for almost two weeks. Morale was not low, but sheer fatigue had left the men hollow-eyed and testy. On the first few nights, the exhilaration of danger and the hope of early relief had cancelled out weariness. The 182 men guarding an expanse which required a thousand for properly rotated watches all felt they could get what rest they needed and restore their stamina once Fannin and his four hundred men got there. It was only as hope dimmed that the nights began to seem endless. Will power alone kept eyes open, senses alert. They had no coffee in the Alamo; whatever other stimulants they might have salvaged had long since been consumed.

The startling hush late in the afternoon of March 5 seemed like a blessed respite—at last a chance to grab a few hours' sleep in the merciful silence. Huddled against the icy walls at their posts, their hands cold on their rifles, they tried to stay out of the sweep of the north wind as they yielded to long-denied rest. For Travis the silence was ominous. He could only wonder what explosion, what storm, would follow it.

At two o'clock that afternoon, Santa Anna had summoned his staff for the decision he had delayed making the day before. Handsomer than most, taller at five feet ten inches than his compatriots, the General cut an imposing figure. Now he spoke with excited conviction of the morrow's victory. Nevertheless his decision to attack was opposed by Generals Castrillon, Cós, and other officers, who wished to wait for two twelve-pound cannon due with another detachment on Monday. Thus far their cannon had opened only one breach in the Alamo's outer walls, a slight and unpromising chink in the northeast pocket of the north wall bounding the large open square inside the fortress. Further bombardment, Cós and Castrillon contended, would open up the walls and make the assault that much easier.

Santa Anna, supported by General Ramirez y Sesma and Colonel Almonte, disregarded such advice. There was no need to wait. They had ladders for scaling the walls. His troops, rested from the rigors of their severe march, would never be readier. Santa Anna announced full and specific details, worked out, for the most part, by General Castrillon. The brilliant Spaniard, though he had refused earlier to serve his commander in his mock marriage, had performed a far more valuable—and appropriate—service.

The secret orders to the staff fixed four o'clock in the morning of the following day, Sunday, March 6, as the time to spring the trap. Four columns of infantry, one from each point of the compass, would simultaneously race for the walls, equipped with axes, crowbars, and scaling ladders. The four commanders of the attacking columns were assigned seconds, in case of death or disability. General Cós was to lead the column attacking from the south, a difficult approach since the chapel and its high walls constituted the Texans' best protection. On his left, Colonel Jose Maria Romero would command the assault from the west. On the north Colonel Francisco Duque had charge, Colonel Juan Morales on the east. The cavalry, under the command of General Ramirez y Sesma, had a double assignment: stationed in the rear of the advancing troops, it was to discourage and prevent desertion or flight of any Mexican soldiers, and was to cut off any attempted Texan escape. Santa Anna himself was to command the reserve, made up of the battalion of engineers and the light companies of the other batallions, though he turned over direct orders to Colonel Augustin Amat. Santa Anna named himself successor to General Cós in case the latter fell.

The instructions were precise and full: "The time has come to strike a decisive blow upon the enemy occupying the Fortress of the Alamo. Consequently, His Excellency, the General in Chief, has decided that tomorrow at 4 o'clock A.M., the columns shall be stationed at musket-shot distance from the first entrenchments, ready for the charge, which shall commence, at a signal given with a bugle, from the Northern Battery."

Twenty-eight ladders for escalade were to be distributed among the four columns. "The men carrying the ladders will sling their guns on their shoulders, to be enabled to place the ladders wherever they may be required." Overcoats and blankets were forbidden, as hindrances to speed; commanders were instructed to see that the men wore either *huaraches* or shoes and that they had "the chin straps of their caps down." The troops were to turn in to sleep at dark, in order to be in readiness to move into appointed positions at midnight. The horses of the cavalry were to be saddled at 3 A.M.

The General in Chief concluded: "The honor of the nation being interested in this engagement against the bold and lawless foreigners who are opposing us, His Excellency expects that every man will do his duty, and exert himself to give a day of glory to the country, and of gratification to the Supreme Government, who will know how to reward the distinguished deeds of the brave soldiers of the Army of Operations."

One reward the government was offering was of recent origin and copied from Napoleon. In January, 1836, the Secretary of War, General Jose Maria Tornel, had decreed the establishing of a Mexican Legion of Honor, a device Santa Anna needed in order to attract recruits. Participation in the war on Texas was a requirement for this supreme honor. The cross which was to be awarded—silver for the soldiers, for the officers gold—would be engraved:

"Honor, Valor and Country." The Grand Cross, with a crown of laurel centered between the five radiants, was to be worn with a red-bordered band of honor across the right and left shoulders.

But Santa Anna also resorted to a more practical and immediate stimulant. He supplied his forces with liberal drafts of *aguardiente*, Mexican firewater, to instill the extra ounce of bravery just before the attack.

Santa Anna hoped to profit not merely by the surprise of this all-out maneuver but also by its perfect timing. In the predawn light the Mexican infantrymen rushing to scale the walls would have the cover of semi-darkness. But once there, they would be able to see well enough to pursue their advantage in the battle against men barely roused from their first deep sleep in a fortnight. He sought the moment when that sleep, so desperately fought off for days, would be at its heaviest.

The Texans, meanwhile, with three sentries posted outside the walls, slept fitfully. One man within the fort remained awake, watching the fires. Once again silence and shadow were the realities inside the mission-fortress.

SLEEP WAS the last thing possible for the Mexican army. By eleven o'clock, infantry, cavalry, and some artillery had been ordered into position. On the cold ground the soldiers waited for the alert from their officers, prey to the north wind sweeping from the Polar Cap down the unresisting eastern slope of the Rockies. They were learning the truth of the Texas proverb: "If it is cold with us, it freezes; if it is hot, it melts; if it is rain, it pours."

A young Mexican private, in a letter written next day

to his brother to describe the awesome events, wrote that after taking their places before the walls at about 3 A.M., they had to remain flat on their stomachs another two hours. *"Caramba!"* he writes. "It was cold!" More than one soldier that night regretted General Santa Anna's orders depriving them of overcoats and blankets.

Santa Anna himself was in a restless state of agitation. He had by this time taken personal command of the Mexican reserve, stationing nearby him the regimental bands. In the darkness, the town and the river lay opposite him; he and the fortress were on the sunrise side of town.

It was late that night, according to his Negro cook, Ben, that he ordered Ben to prepare refreshments and coffee and to keep them ready all night. Ben thought his master cast down and discontented. Certainly he did not retire at all, and drank but little of the coffee Ben served him. He went out at about eleven o'clock with Colonel Almonte, and did not return till 3 A.M. Upon returning, he told Almonte that if the Alamo garrison could be brought to surrender, he would be content. All his summonses had been treated with disdain. He did not see any alternative to sending the enemy, all unprepared, to meet their God. He could no longer continue wasting the military resources of the nation.

In the meantime he spared a thought for the Mexican troops who would be killed and wounded, summoning the San Fernando parish priest, Don Refugio de la Garza, to be ready to tend the injured at a temporary fortification set up on Protero Street. With the curate would be the political chief, Don Ramón Músquiz, and the mayor of Béxar, Don Francisco Ruiz. Santa Anna looked with extreme suspicion upon the latter. Perhaps he knew that four days before, Ruiz's father, as a delegate to the Texan Convention, had signed his name to the declaration of independence at Washington-on-the-Brazos. To this "neutral" *alcalde*, Francisco Ruiz, would go the assignment of assembling the Texan dead and burning them. As soon as the storming started these San Antonio leaders were to proceed toward the walls to help give aid to the Mexican casualties.

The exact time of Santa Anna's signal for attack is not known. Reports vary—from three o'clock to five or a little later. Santa Anna's second-in-command, General Filisola, stated that the Mexican troops were stationed at 2 A.M., in accord with Santa Anna's instructions. According to Ben, Santa Anna left his headquarters about 4 A.M., with other members of the staff. It was several moments before Ben heard the tremendous outburst of the bull-throated Texan eighteen-pounder. By that time the final battle for the Alamo was under way.

Three startling and separate sounds roused the Texans into wakefulness. They occurred almost simultaneously.

A blast from a bugle lifted the Mexican infantry to its feet from the cold ground. At once there began from each of four columns on the four sides of the fortress a wild rush of humanity. The piercing bugle blast was as nothing compared to this second sound—the drumming of thousands of feet on the hard ground. Beside Santa Anna there now poured forth into the frozen air the third sound, most fearful of all. Santa Anna's regimental band burst forth with the notes of an ancient Moorish battle march, the famed *deguello*, signal that no quarter would be given. It was the musical equivalent of the red flag of no mercy that Santa Anna had planted atop the bell tower of San

Fernando Church. In the present dark, the flag could not be seen. But its meaning was not forgotten.

Once again Santa Anna was hearing this somber and fierce bugle cry of the *deguello*. Always it had haunted him with its Moorish menace of brutality. He was descended from Romany stock, and the *deguello*, with its dark, modulated succession of low-C notes, awakened echoes in him of age-old savagery. The *deguello* had become his personal battle signature since it had first blown fortune to him twelve years before at Vera Cruz. Though he had changed sides many times since then, his battle cry was still the same.

It was an alien cry when the Moors first sounded it in Spain long ago and the Spanish had first named it, after the verb that meant "to slit the throat"—*degollar*. Now General Antonio Lopez de Santa Anna was in a very special way alien, too. Four days earlier the Texan declaration of independence at Washington-on-the-Brazos had made Santa Anna, whether he knew it or not, an alien in San Antonio de Béxar.

The Texan sentries posted outside the Alamo must have been bayoneted almost at once; they gave no outcry. The first alarm, according to Travis's slave boy, Joe, came from Travis himself: "Come on, men! The Mexicans are upon us! And we will give them hell!" The Mexicans were there, indeed, 2,500 front-line effectives against the Alamo garrison of 182. A large reserve was in back and ready to intercept fugitives from either side. The giant push was on. Cannon balls began to rain down on the fortress from all sides.

Travis, with rifle and sword and followed by the faithful Joe, raced seventy yards to his battle station at the fortress's most vulnerable point. He stood by the twelve-pounder mounted on a platform near the northwest corner, covering that single breach in the north wall which the Mexican artillery had been able to make in the Texans' fortifications.

Davy Crockett and his Tennessee boys were stationed on the southeast side of the open court, guarding the heavily entrenched but low stockade wall that ran from the chapel westward to join the south wall. They were in the best position to guard the main entrance gate in the middle of the wall.

Jim Bonham was atop the chapel, commanding three twelve-pound cannon. From debris within the church, the Texans had made a ramp to a stockade platform at the very back of the apse and placed the cannon so they could fire in three directions over the roofless church walls —one south, one east, one north. Bonham could pivot his cannon, but most of the others in the fort had been installed in a way which allowed little maneuverability. They could not be traversed downward, and were useless against the Mexican infantry once it had reached the base of the outer walls.

Feeble but armed, Jim Bowie lay on his cot in the southwest corner baptistry of the chapel. Davy Crockett had provided him with a brace of loaded pistols. Bowie, who had not recognized Juan Seguin on February 29 when Seguin had asked permission to take his horse, was only intermittently conscious now. The men who had cared for him earlier could no longer be spared. In the chapel, Bowie was as safe as anyone could be at this moment in the Alamo. And he was with the women who had come inside the Alamo to look after him. He had rejected their care at first, saying they might catch his illness. But there was a greater danger now than tuberculosis. Sheeted ghost though Bowie was, his presence still was a comfort.

Though startled, the small Texas garrison rallied in a breath and met the first assault on the walls with supreme success. The cannon fire caught scores of Mexicans racing towards the walls. Accurate rifle fire made Mexican casualties so heavy at the start that the Texans got an unexpected respite while Mexican infantry was being regrouped and a second attack organized.

A new burst of hope spread through the Texans. If they could rally again to decimate the troops trying a second assault, Santa Anna might call a halt. He was paying a fearful price, as the moans and screams below the walls testified.

Santa Anna had counted on surprise—his chief weapon in all his campaigns—and on the overpowering effect of a frontal assault from four directions. The losses he was receiving had been expected. If victorious here, he could fill his ranks with a thousand recruits from the neutral Mexicans of San Antonio, potentially his chief reservoir for conscription. But he could not enforce this conscription until he had destroyed the last Texan at the Alamo.

The roar and flash of cannonade, the orange fire of exploding shot, the throat-shattering battle cries outside the Alamo now thickened as the first attack was repulsed. Disorder threatened the success of the assault.

When the bugle first sounded, the troops under General Cós had heard their leader shout "Forward!" and grabbing their axes, guns, picks, crowbars, and spikes, had sped to protection at the base of the Alamo walls, protection at least from the cannon, which could not be deflected for firing at close range. But here the danger from the Texas rifles was equally great.

In this duel of marksmanship the Texans also had their difficulty. The Alamo walls were not crenellated and had no bastions allowing a man to shoot without exposing his body. Once the Mexicans had raced under the shadow of the twelve-foot walls, the marksmen had to stand on top of the wall to take aim, offering themselves to the Mexican rear guard as easy targets.

Inside the chapel walls, twelve-year-old Enrique Esparza begged for a gun so he could fight beside his father. The boy and his mother watched thirty-three-year-old Gregorio Esparza hold the torch to the touch-hole of one of the twelve-pounders directed by Jim Bonham. The cannoneers stood back from the recoil as the big gun roared.

Denied his plea, Gregorio's son wept. He pointed out that other boys there were grabbing guns from the dead men. But there were better shots than he in need of firing pieces. He had to give in. Fifteen miles away, one of Enrique's boyhood friends, José Rodriguez, was watching the battle from the flat rooftop of a hacienda where he and his mother had found refuge. His father, Ambrosio Rodriguez, also fighting with the Texans, was away on a scouting mission at Gonzales. Even from here José and his mother could see the flame and flash of gunfire.

The first man to die in the storming of the fort was a shoemaker by trade and a Mexican soldier by conscription. His name was Juan Basquez. He had ten more years to serve in Santa Anna's army before he could return to his home in Durango. A year before, he had tried to desert and had been fittingly punished—sentenced to ten years' service without pay. In addition, he was compelled to run a gauntlet of troopers beating him violently with the iron ramrods of their rifles. Somehow Juan Basquez lived through it, and then survived the march into Texas. Unlike the two thousand who had deserted between Saltillo and Béxar, he had lost his chance. Hemmed in now, in the cold dawn light of March 6, by a ring of bayonets and the flats of swords behind him, he died, perhaps gratefully, in the first volley.

The Texans knew they would lose to sheer force of numbers if ever the Mexicans got over the outer walls. One hundred and eighty-two men, well protected, could take a mighty toll of several thousand attackers. At least in the beginning. But the walls must not be breached. So it was that the fight for the outer walls became the crucial part of the battle. But though more men fell in this initial assault, it was neither the fiercest nor the longest engagement of this cold March 6 day.

AFTER THE FIRST SURGE failed, the Mexican staff reassorted its battalions with clear and resolute purpose. They too saw the crucial necessity of pouring men over the walls before morale crumbled, before losses mounted too high. All possible provisions had been made to guarantee that this attack would not fail.

Primary in this insurance was the massing of Mexican cavalry behind the men who were to scale the walls. Desertion, fugitive retreat, escape, all were effectively cut off. For the second attack the circle of cavalry enclosing and shortening the battle area was further tightened.

It was a wise precaution. A young Mexican soldier wrote that the distance he and his fellows had to run after the first bugle blast was short, but "the fire from the enemy's cannon was fearful; we fell back more; *more than forty men fell around me in a few moments....* The whole scene was one of extreme terror."

On the first wave Colonel Francisco Duque, in command of the north column, was so gravely wounded that in the confusion he was trampled to death by his own men, spurred relentlessly from behind. Such must have happened to many another. With their comrades falling all around them, the Mexicans must have felt a wild surge of response to the incessant reminder of the *deguello* that no mercy was to be granted. General Santa Anna had reminded his staff over and over, repeating it because Urrea and Castrillon and others tended to disagree: *"En esta guerra no habrá prisoneros—* In this war there will be no prisoners...."

Now, with staggering casualties, the Mexican generals could risk no delay. Some of the units had already lost nearly half their men. Too many had already dropped their muskets in amazement at the Texans' fire, screaming, *"Diablos! Diablos!"* The second charge must follow swiftly on the rout of the first.

So effective was the rain of grape and musket balls which the Alamo's "devil" defenders had cascaded upon the Mexicans that two commanders wavered and, intentionally or not, changed their plans. Instead of remaining on the south side, the column repulsed there shifted toward the western salient; and the column on the east, in the excitement and rout of the first moments of battle, drifted toward union with the attacking column on the north. The fluidity proved to be a boon to the Mexican side. The two shifts in position rendered useless the fixed Texas cannon pointing south and east. At the same time, the column on the west moved up toward the north, further reducing the expanse of enemy target. The Texans had no choice but to stand on top of the walls, where, as General Filisola noted, "they could not survive a moment." Gradually the Mexican forces were, more through accident than design, converging on the one breach in the Alamo walls, that on the north. It was here that Travis stood.

Against the second wave of attack the Texas artillery was much less effective than against the first. But in both waves, the Mexicans themselves were penalized in the use of heavy cannonade by their own tactics. Because of the planned rushes from four directions, the danger of artillery firing over the enemy and into the opposite columns of Mexicans was great. Filisola claims the Mexicans lost more men in each other's gunfire than they did to Texas marksmanship. Despite this, the second assault, which occurred around 5:30 A.M. and only minutes after the first, started strong.

The Texas cannon kept up a constant thunder. Santa Anna's men were so excited that their vociferous shouting vexed even their commander. He would have taken the Texans by surprise, he asserted in his memoirs, but for the idiotic war whoops from one of the attacking columns.

Despite this new alignment of Mexican troops and the concentration of force on the north sector—the one defended by Travis—Texan fire succeeded in repulsing the second attack. No scaling ladder stood in place long enough to permit entry over the walls. The Texans picked off top man after top man, tumbling him onto the men below; on some occasions ladders were toppled over with such violence as to break the necks of men caught in the collisions.

By now the sky was streaked with early red. Similar

streaks began appearing on the walls, the ground, on sleeves and chests. The calmest man, the Mexicans reported, was the Texan in buckskin who wore the peculiar cap. Two Mexican captains, both of whom pronounced his name "Kwokety," praised Davy Crockett's composure as well as his skill. Captain Rafael Soldana of the Tampico battalion described him standing up to reload his gun, indifferent to enemy fire, while he poured scorn on the enemy with his great voice before leveling Old Betsy for another kill.

It was possible now in the half-light to make out the colors of the Mexican uniforms. They had changed markedly since Daniel Cloud first saw them from the San Fernando bell tower. The blue cotton jackets with the white shoulder belts crossed at the breast and the white trousers of the Mexican infantry were stained red with blood, blackened by smoke. Their leather or felt black shakos bearing pompons and metallic trimmings rose above faces almost as black with dirt and grime. Some battalions wore worsted shoulder knots of red, blue, and green, bursts of color lost in the orange flash of gunfire.

As for the uniforms of the defenders, they were of every kind and none at all—buckskin hunting shirt, blanket coat, remnants of costume from the troops of the New Orleans Grays, and the rags and tags of handmade clothing. Besides the coon-skin cap, the Texans had headgear of every description. Their commander, however, was dressed in a style worthy of his position. William Barret Travis had on January 21 ordered himself a uniform: gray swallow-tail coat, pantaloons and forage cap, with facings, stripes, and bands of black. He always carried a sword at his side.

It was this group of volunteers, half in rags, that

turned back the second attack as successfully as they had stopped the first. They endured a third swift attack as well, but this one they could not keep outside the walls.

THE WEAK CENTER of the northern wall, opened two days before by Mexican fire, was the point finally breached by the Mexicans under the command of General Juan Amador. It was this breach that deprived General Cós, on the south, of the credit he sought; this breach that ended the first act of the battle on the morning of March 6 and ushered in the second.

It was a victory of sheer numbers; no wall could stand against an army ready to sacrifice thousands. Pouring flood-strong through the northeast wall, the Mexican infantry took quick positions behind segments of blasted rock, behind dead bodies, in angles or recesses. Most of the men had to remain in the open, and following the example of the first ones inside the walls, knelt quickly on one knee to fire swiftly at the nearest target. Single combat with rifle, bayonet, and knife became the pattern. Now it was by uniform and weapon that each side distinguished the enemy. The Texans had no bayonets but they did have bowie knives. They still manned one or two cannon stations that kept blasting away. Half the walls of the convent barracks were split apart. The crashing noise of shattering walls, the human cries, the roar of guns were thunderous in the small area. If the bells of San Fernando church had rung at six o'clock that morning, they could not have been heard.

With the enemy inside the inner court of the Alamo, the Texans had to alter their strategy. The men on the outer walls now had to shoot in all directions. And they were shot at from every angle. They had to fire over the walls, protect themselves from shots out front, from shots in back and from below, while trying to halt the stampede of men tumbling through the breach, as Travis's Joe put it, "like sheep." The guns required reloading after each shot and now their chief use was for clubbing the enemy to death.

For Davy Crockett even that was impossible. A Mexican shot had broken his right arm; he began firing with his left till his gun was broken off at the stock and the gunbarrel fell to the floor. Crockett drew his knife, and fought with his dirk in the thick of the musket fire, breathing the sweetish, sickening odor of burnt gunpowder.

The Texans had only one recourse: to seek refuge, to shut themselves inside the barracks rooms against the walls, inside the two-story former convent, or inside the Alamo chapel. They fought *mano-a-mano* with swords, tomahawks, knives, and bayonets as they leaped from their posts atop the walls and barricaded themselves inside the barracks for a momentary advantage. The leap from the wall itself became a weapon, to the surprise of General Filisola: "They fired upon our men in the act of jumping down onto the square or court of the fort."

Not all leaped down for hand-to-hand combat. At battery position on the frame scaffoldings or earth mounds some of the Texas cannoneers labored their guns into position to fire down into the court. One particular twelve-pound cannon on the west wall did great damage, according to one Mexican general. As with the others, however, the cannoneers were quickly picked off as Mexican sharpshooters took aim from a dozen directions. As soon as a cannon was abandoned, or all its men dead, the Mexicans seized and turned it—together with the few light cannon they had brought in—on the doors of the barracks rooms.

Their deadliest gun was the Texans' own eighteen-pounder. They turned it on the long barracks, breaking apart door after door, shattering the sandbag or cowhide barricades inside the rooms by the strength of cannon shot. The doors and few windows of the Alamo buildings were barricaded with sandbags as tall as a man, but to no avail. Once the rooms were opened, they were stormed, one after the other, and taken at the point of bayonet.

Sergeant Becerra worked with one Mexican group pointing a captured cannon at the south door of the long barracks. This eight-pounder was doubly charged with grape and canister and fired twice. The Mexicans entered through the blown-away door frame to find fifteen Texan corpses.

Elsewhere the Texans were killed by bayonets in their backs while fighting their adversaries in front with bowie knives. No one involved in the fighting would be spared, not even the youngest.

Galba Fuqua, seventeen, was probably the youngest fighter among the Texans. Early in the battle, his jaws were broken by enemy fire. Leaving his post by the walls for a moment he ran to the chapel where Mrs. Dickinson and the other women had sought asylum. Young Fuqua gestured toward Mrs. Dickinson, pointed to his jaws and tried desperately to tell her something. It may have been a warning or a message for his mother and father. Or it may have been a hopeless plea for help. She could not understand what he tried to say. He made the effort again, this time holding his jaws in place with his hands. But his straining to make the sounds was futile. Sadly Mrs. Dickinson shook her head in noncomprehension. The boy focused all he had to say in a pathetic last entreating glance, turned and raced back to the walls. Mrs. Dickinson never saw him alive again.

THE CANNON manned by William Barret Travis near the northwest wall was the scene of one of the first Texas deaths. Perhaps the first Texan killed in the Alamo was Travis himself. Slumped over his twelve-pounder, he was found with a single shot straight through the head. The fact that he had only one wound, and a clean one at that, has given rise to a conjecture that Travis committed suicide.

The evidence is a little roundabout. Two Mexicans, Anselmo Borgarra and Antonio Perez, San Antonio civilians who had sped to Gonzales to inform Captain Juan Seguin of the fall of the Alamo, reported to Sam Houston that Travis had shot himself through the head when he realized at last that the floodtide of Mexican soldiers could no longer be stopped. By Santa Anna's own reckoning, the assault started about 5 A.M.; the plaza was seized by 8 A.M. Did Travis feel after several hours of fighting that he could no longer help his men? Was it more honorable to give the example of dying by one's own hand rather than by the enemy's?

This version, which is not necessarily inconsistent with Travis's temperament, is given further weight by the testimony of Don Francisco Ruiz, assigned the task of burning the Texan bodies. Santa Anna, Ruiz said, wanted to be shown the bodies of Travis, Crockett, and Bowie.

Travis was found first, where he lay across the gun carriage of the cannon at the breached wall, "shot only through the forehead." He had no other sign of battle injury by sword or bayonet.

A friend of Travis's, furthermore, Andrew Briscoe, in making an account of the fall of the Alamo to the *New Orleans Post and Union*, told the editor, "The brave and gallant Travis, to prevent his falling into the hands of the enemy, shot himself."

And yet the one person who was both there to see it and lived to tell of it gave a totally different report. Travis's servant boy Joe, liberated by Santa Anna and summoned before the new ad interim Texas government to give an eye-witness account of the battle, said that his master was shot and fell backward on the sloping ramp where his cannon was placed. Travis had just enough strength left to sit up once, at which moment General Mora of the Mexican advance rushed upon him with a bayonet. Travis summoned what life was left in him, lunged with his last breath and sank his sword straight into the general. He was pierced himself while piercing the other, the two officers expiring together. Joe added that when he saw his master die, he ran and hid in one of the rooms of the long barracks. Travis's last words to his men, says J. J. Linn in his memoirs, were in Spanish: *"No rendirse, muchachos."* Don't surrender, boys. . . .

Travis's essential character would seem to argue against his suicide. He and his men had known for days now that no help was coming in time to save them. All they were living for was to make the enemy pay a price that would turn victory into actual defeat. Their one aim was to kill as many adversaries as possible. This was also their glory. Fate had simplified their task for them. It was no more complicated than this: the enemy they destroyed would never fight other Texans; the time they made the enemy lose would secure the solidarity of their countrymen, and allow new defenses to form.

"Travis," Sergeant Becerra wrote, "died like a brave man with his rifle in his hand at the back of a cannon."

His clean wound may well prove only that his was one of the first Texan deaths. In the headlong rush to secure entrance over the walls, and before the carnage of close combat began, the enemy soldiers did not have the chance to practice on him the mutilation they did on others. They had not yet passed from warfare into orgy. That part of the battle was just beginning.

THE TEXAN RESISTANCE was a drama in four acts that morning which lasted not much longer than a full-length tragedy on the stage. The first act of defense was the attempt to hold the walls against the Mexican assaults. The second act occurred in the courtyard area, their plaza, where the battle was joined hand to hand. The last two acts were in a sense indoors—the first in the barracks, the last in the Alamo chapel.

The third act, and the most bitterly fought with the greatest number of casualties amongst the Texans, was the retreat into the walled redoubt of the convent barracks. This same two-story stone building once had heard the soft murmurs of confession and rosaries and later had housed the Flying Company of the Alamo of Parras.

The Texans had carefully equipped these last resorts for defense. Most of the rooms had interior parapets just inside the doorway, parapets built of two frames of bear or cowhides stretched on poles, with the inner cavity thickly mounded with rammed earth. At long last, by means of this construction, the outnumbered Texans were able to fire at the enemy from behind considerable protection.

Where they were not blasted out of their refuges by cannon fire, the Texans stacked up the enemy dead in great numbers as the Mexicans tried to gain entry. But here again, individual bravery could not stand for long against superior numbers and greater weapons. Room after room fell to the invader.

Davy Crockett was still outdoors. Travis had assigned him the most difficult spot of all, a south stretch of ground between the mighty-walled chapel and the south wall proper. Strictly speaking, he had no solid protection at all. A picket fence, stockade type, formed the connection between the chapel and the south wall of stone. But this vulnerable fifty yards had been carefully strengthened by Green B. Jameson. A strong earth parapet backed the picket fence and Crockett had been assigned four cannon, all four-pounders at this entrenchment. "Just give me my place to defend," he told Travis on the first day, "and me and my Tennessee boys will hold it."

The place was a difficult one to hold, but an appropriate one for the man who had always urged that the battle be carried against the Mexicans outside the walls. "I hate to be hemmed in," Davy had often protested.

Now, like Travis, Crockett died outdoors, where he wished to be. When the firing was over, he and his men were found at their assigned post near the stockade fence. In his hand was "Old Betsy," his favorite rifle, the inscription down the length of the barrel reading "Presented by the young men of Philadelphia, to the Honorable David Crockett." In mute testimony to a man whose marksmanship was legendary, the greatest concentration of Mexican bodies is said to have been found around Crockett's body. Santa Anna's cook, Ben, said the fifty-year-old frontiersman was surrounded by "no less than sixteen Mexican corpses" and that one lay across his body with the "huge knife of Davy buried in the Mexican's bosom to the hilt." Travis's Joe reported that "Crockett and a few of his friends were found together with twenty-four of the enemy dead around them." Others set the figure at seventeen.

The very last act of the Alamo drama took place in the only building that stands today, the Alamo chapel.

Though in ruins and largely filled with debris, the chapel, with its four-foot-thick walls, twenty-two and a half feet high, was still the strongest building in the mission. The three twelve-pounders that Green B. Jameson had mounted and that Jim Bonham commanded on the sloping ramp of the east wall kept up a steady fire during most of the battle in spite of the shortage of ammunition. But it was not as an offensive position that the chapel was to be used in the final hour; as it had given sanctuary in the days of the Indian wars, it was to be used for sanctuary again.

Into the chapel now withdrew the remnants of the Texas army. Here were already gathered the six or seven women in the Alamo, the few children, the two Negro servant-cooks for Travis and Bowie, Joe and Sam. By most reports, Bowie himself was sequestered in a side room, the baptistry.

By this time the outcome was no longer, if it had ever been, in doubt. But here again the Mexican troops met stubborn resistance. In particular they encountered the fire of Bonham, Gregorio Esparza, and the other cannoneers— under the over-all command of Almeron Dickinson on the east wall.

When the breach had been made in the north wall, Dickinson's men had wheeled their cannon around and trained the guns on the west. By now, however, the cannoneers had no balls left to fire. They were plugging their guns with rocks, scraps of cast iron, broken pieces of chain. One of the first Mexican officers to enter the chapel door when it was finally blasted open saw one of his men topple over at his side, his skull blown off by one of the guns on the ramp. Bonham, Dickinson, Esparza, Jacob Walker, and the other cannoneers became major targets. A Mexican officer trained a force of muskets on them. Bonham fell across the carriage of the gun on the north side. Walker, unable any longer to fire his cannon, leaped from the ramp and dashed to the side of Mrs. Dickinson in one of the small side rooms. Gregorio Esparza fell next, fell and rolled from the ramp, his body broken when it hit the ground.

It was in the chapel, too, that Jim Bowie died. In a sense, this was his third death. The spirit had gone out of him in 1833 when his wife and children died; the fall from the scaffold had rendered him semiconscious, half alive. Now he waited in the small baptistry in the southwest corner of the Alamo, the women who had followed him into the Alamo attending him, the brace of pistols left by Davy Crockett's men ready at his side. It was with these, and the bowie knife that never left him, that Bowie hoped to take as many Mexicans with him as time and strength would allow.

When the Mexicans at last burst into the baptistry, they thought Bowie a ghost, with pale face and emaciated form to match. But the Alamo's co-commander was not yet dead. Rallying with superb effort, he began firing at the enemy, holding his knife in reserve for those who came near. When at last the small room fell silent, it was said that Mexican bodies filled the doorway. In death Jim Bowie had recovered some of the strength and courage of his earlier years.

The Texans still alive in the chapel were now more than ever determined not to yield. They had an additional reason for fighting to defend the church. Their store of powder, captured from General Cós in December, had been cached in a northern room of the chapel which still had a roof and was the least vulnerable to enemy gunfire. By agreement, the last man alive among the Texans was to light a torch to this cache of powder. Their hope was that this explosion would blow a lot of Mexicans to hell, with luck maybe even Santa Anna.

It was Major Robert Evans who made the decision that the time had come to obliterate the fort as the Texans had been obliterated in it. Though the battle was clearly lost, he had to weigh the lives of the women and children in the church against the agreed-upon plan to try to blow up the Mexican horde. In the chapel area before him were Mrs. Dickinson and her baby, the several Mexican women and their children, the Negro servant boys of Travis and Bowie. Here were also the dead bodies of the Texan cannoneers stretched over the carriage of their guns on the improvised earth ramp. His torch flaring, Major Evans made a dash for the powder magazine.

But the pounding of cannon balls had breached the

chapel's barred doors and the Mexicans streamed in before Major Evans chose his moment. Arm raised to hurl the fire into the powder, he was shot down on the run before he could touch off the explosion. He fell face downward on the earthen floor.

This was probably the last act of attempted aggression by any living Texan at the Alamo. Like the support for the beleaguered garrison which was now gathering rapidly in the settlements to the east, it came too late.

ANOTHER TEXAN was still alive. Jacob Walker, the gunner from Nacogdoches who had remained by his cannon as part of Jim Bonham's company until his wounds had put him out of the battle, had made his way to the side of Mrs. Dickinson in one of the chapel side rooms. Perhaps he hoped like young Galba Fuqua and many another that she would be spared to carry messages to the living. During the siege he had often talked with her about his wife and four children. His cousin Asa was also at the Alamo.

Asa Walker had come to Texas from Tennessee the year before. He was in a hurry, and had written his good friend, William Gant: "I take the responsibility of taking your overcoat and gun—your gun they would have anyhow & I might as well have it as anyone else.... If you can overtake me you can take your gun and I will trust to chance." He concludes with an apology and signs himself "your friend at heart. A. WALKER." Gant joined him and they made the trip to Texas together. Now Asa lay dead.

When the Mexicans found Jacob he was beside Mrs. Dickinson, trying to give her a message. In his agony Walker pleaded for his life. It was in vain. Mrs. Dickinson reported that the Mexicans "tossed his body on their bayonets as a farmer would toss a bundle of hay."

Walker's death may well have been the last one in the Alamo.

GREGORIO ESPARZA, whose three sons and small daughter were now clutching their mother's dress, had been happy with his life in San Antonio. He had once noted: "Of food we had not overmuch—chile and beans, beans and chile ... but there was time to eat and sleep and look at growing plants."

When Gregorio Esparza lifted his twelve-year-old son through the Alamo chapel window on the first day of the siege, his friend John W. Smith had already left with Dr. Sutherland on their scout to Gonzales. About that same time Gregorio's brother, a sergeant in Santa Anna's army, was marching behind the Mexican regimental bands into the Military Plaza of San Antonio de Béxar. The Esparza family had split over the question of Mexican dictatorship.

It was Gregorio's wife who had insisted that she and the children come with him into the Alamo. Her husband, despite John W. Smith's urging, was uncertain. Mrs. Esparza, shepherding her children, had told him: "I will stay by your side."

She was by his side now, where he had fallen from the ramp along the east wall. The children beside her had also witnessed the last moments of Gregorio Esparza. Though all the men in the Alamo were dead, the guns continued firing. The shots and shells kept tearing great holes in the walls, sawing out jagged segments in both the convent building and the chapel. But the mother acted as though she did not hear. She held Gregorio Esparza's body next to her breast and wept. She stayed there, at her husband's side, until the officers came and ordered mother and children to the Ramón Músquiz house in San Antonio to await the arrival of General Santa Anna.

Mrs. Dickinson, in the chapel side room, was also ordered to the Músquiz house. It was where she had been living when the siege began, where on the first day of the siege she had stood waiting for her husband.

GENERAL SANTA ANNA took no direct part in the battle but supervised it from a small adobe house in the street leading directly south from the Alamo, about fifty yards east of the bridge and 500 yards from the fortress walls. He had stationed around him all the regimental bands, which played lustily during the assault. When the din and uproar inside the walls seemed to halt, at about 9 A.M., Santa Anna summoned his escort of music and began a triumphal approach to the south gates. He had timed his entry badly. A Texan sharpshooter, still possessing shot and still alive on a parapet near the top of the wall, fired a last bullet; it whistled over the general's head. He, and his music, returned to cover until he got an urgent message from General Castrillon stating that the Texans were positively finished. Castrillon needed the commander in chief. Though the Texans were dead, the firing had not totally ceased.

Two Mexican testimonies describe this final orgy of violence on the part of the victorious Mexican soldiers. Felix Nuñez, who fought with Santa Anna, said his comrades in the moment of victory "became uncontrollable and, owing to the darkness of the building and the smoke of the battle, fell to killing one another, not being able to distinguish friend from foe." Mexican generals, he said, had urgently informed Santa Anna of this. *El Presidente* mounted a wall, expecting his presence to stop the carnage. It did not end, Nuñez said, until all the buglers sounded a retreat.

Enrique Esparza, writing years later, confirms this, and adds an interesting detail. After the Mexican soldiers had herded into a corner of the chapel all the women and children not killed in the onslaught, they continued to fire at the bodies of the men who had defended the Alamo. "For fully a quarter of an hour," Enrique adds, "they kept firing after all the defenders had been slain and their corpses were lying still."

The Mexicans had seen their comrades, their kin, fall in stacks during the first two assaults. The walls of the fort had magnified the tumult of explosion, shouting, and destruction. Mutilated bodies, pools of blood, and the stench of powder and of death mesmerized the men on both sides.

More than 500 bodies now lay in the blood of the Alamo courtyard, many of them still clenched together, one hand at a throat, the other holding fast to its sword or pistol or gun. General Santa Anna gave instructions to have every face wiped clean of grime and smoke—he did not wish to confuse Mexican and Texan bodies.

The very nature of the combat had compelled this slaughter. Mexican losses had been unbelievably high. At the end of the third charge the Tolucca battalion, under the command of General Morales, had had only 130 of its

830 men alive. The prodding of the cavalry in the first and second assaults had caused the Mexican infantry to drive forward over the dead bodies of their comrades, crushing the wounded.

And as Santa Anna had decreed, there were no combatant prisoners taken. Mrs. Dickinson and the other women and their children and the presumably noncombatant servant boys, Joe and Sam, were the only survivors. The much-debated report of Santa Anna's secretary, Ramon Martinez Caro, confirms that these were the only ones who lived. It also implies that there might have been more had the Mexicans allowed surrender.

Caro, after admitting many previous falsehoods in order to be now believed, claimed that after all the fighting was over, five Texans were discovered hidden away under mattresses in one of the far barracks rooms against the west wall. These men, Caro states, were promptly brought into the presence of Santa Anna, who was outraged that they had not been put to death at once. General Castrillon, who had been horrified at the mutilations thus far committed, bespoke mercy on their behalf. Santa Anna treated this brilliant commander with angry contempt. He turned his back and walked off, leaving the soldier guard which had brought in the Texans to divine his meaning. There was no hesitation. Breaking out of ranks they rushed upon the prisoners and bayoneted them again and again.

Caro insisted that the whole army could vouch for this episode. But by the time it was published, the Mexican leaders were trying frenziedly to transfer guilt for their later defeat to somebody else, and their testimony, like that of Caro, is hardly objective. Caro himself had a score to settle with Santa Anna.

Caro's story rings true only in one respect. In the character of Santa Anna, Caro had captured the very essence of his contempt and cruelty.

Young Enrique Esparza, who had seen Santa Anna dismount in the Plaza the first day of the siege, had revised the splendid impression he had received. The image he saw now included thirteen days of wrath.

It was one of Santa Anna's few relaxed moments. Ramón Músquiz had offered food that morning to the prisoners. Though they were unable to eat, Santa Anna ate bread and meat and drank coffee before them. He was even moved to an impulse of kindness. When told that Gregorio Esparza's brother had fought on the Mexican side, Santa Anna summoned the brother and sent him to separate Gregorio's body from the Texan dead. Gregorio Esparza's body would not be burned. Of all the Texans killed, he alone had a Christian burial.

But the impression that remained with Gregorio's son was that of a cruel man. He said later: "Santa Anna's countenance was a very sinister one. It has haunted me ever since I last saw it, and I will never forget the face or the figure of Santa Anna."

He was still seeing it sixty years after the battle, when he was an old man describing the events of that day.

SUSANNA DICKINSON that day had seen the face of terror. Frantic with concern for the safety of her husband and baby daughter, she had listened to many a last message, received from dying men many a letter and memento to carry back to their families. The Mexicans had taken everything—letters, keepsakes—everything but what the mind hoarded. Sitting in the Músquiz house now, she had only her thoughts and the memory of her dead husband.

Almeron Dickinson had been an ordnance expert in the United States army before he came to Texas but had resigned his commission to become a farmer. He picked first Tennessee, then Texas. He settled in Gonzales as a blacksmith.

Dickinson left Tennessee, it is said, for a rather special reason. He was in love with Susanna Wilkinson but, in a rash moment of anger toward Susanna, had become engaged to one of her friends. To make matters worse, the girl had invited Susanna to be one of the bridesmaids and on the day of the wedding sent Almeron to escort bridesmaid Susanna to the church. It was a mistake. He never came back. Susanna had thought things over, and they eloped that night. They had come to Texas in 1831; Susanna was only thirteen or fourteen when they were married.

Destiny had led them to the Alamo. It was here, during the siege, according to one story, that he lost his life in a leap from the east wall.

The story can hardly be verified, although Sergeant Becerra swore to Captain Reuben Marmaduke Potter of the United States Army that it was true, and Potter believed him. According to Becerra, Dickinson leaped with his daughter in his arms from a point on the east wall where the muddy bottom of the *acequia* would break his fall. Since he was commanding the cannon at the eastern embrasure of the chapel and his wife and daughter were sequestered in the church, he could easily have made his way to get his child and returned to the wall. Some accounts add the detail that he had tied the child to his back.

Whatever the purpose—whether it was to save the life of the child or to meet his wife later in case Santa Anna spared her—Dickinson, according to Becerra's story, never got a chance to carry it out. A shower of Mexican bullets caught him and the child in midair.

Since the child survived the battle along with Mrs. Dickinson, there could be no truth in that aspect of the story. But the exact circumstances of Almeron Dickinson's death—whether by his cannon or at the foot of the wall—must remain a mystery.

CAPTAIN DICKINSON's was not the only death that day that offers a puzzle. The deaths of the three men most closely identified with the Alamo—Crockett, Bowie, and Travis—have strange and absorbing elements of mystery. If it is unthinkable that Travis committed suicide, it is even more so that Crockett escaped. But there were some that said he did.

Perhaps it was the reluctance of those who had felt his power to let Davy Crockett die that created the legend that Crockett surrendered—and escaped to California or Mexico. The larger-than-life quality that made the Mexicans brag that Davy and six of his boys cringed before Santa Anna caused the Americans to claim he had power to outwit death.

There can be no validity to these stories. Ben, Santa Anna's cook, who had often seen Congressman Crockett in Washington, saw him a last time after the battle, his coonskin cap lying at his side. The cap also caught the eye of Mrs. Dickinson as she was led out of the Alamo. "I recognized Colonel Crockett," she reported, "lying dead and mutilated between the church and the two-story barracks; I even remember seeing his peculiar cap by his side."

Of Jim Bowie's death there are a dozen different accounts, most of them prompted by hatred and fear, some prompted by love.

All accounts but one testify to Bowie's final desperate rallying to kill before being killed. Sergeant Becerra, hardly knowing Bowie was ill, claimed "perverse and haughty James Bowie died like a woman, in bed, almost hidden by covers." All others—Mrs. Dickinson, Enrique Esparza, Madam Candelaria who claimed she had accompanied Bowie to the Alamo at the request of Sam Houston—agree that Bowie in his last moments traded his life for more than one of the enemy.

Even Santa Anna expected Bowie to be courageous to the end. When the *generalissimo* passed inspection once the battle was over, he felt a surge of respect for Bowie upon looking at his mutilated body. This man, he said, was too brave to die like a dog. His body should be exempt from burning. But the habit of contempt was too strong. Changing his mind, Santa Anna barked out the command: "*Pues no es cosa, escade!*"

Madam Candelaria, whose various accounts are contradictory, testified she was in Bowie's room when the Mexican soldiers found him. She threw her body over his to protect him, she said, but the Mexicans plunged bayonets over her shoulder. When she walked out of the side room into the chapel, she said the blood on the chapel floor flowed into her shoes. Another survivor, Mrs. Alsbury, reported that the Mexicans tossed Bowie's body on their bayonets "until his blood covered their clothes and dyed them red."

The other stories—that Bowie died in a delirium an hour before the attack or that he was found late in the afternoon still alive and spoke with such eloquence of Texas liberty that his tongue was cut out and his body burned— cannot be credited. The accepted story is the one given, that Bowie was brought into the southwest room of the chapel a day or so before the final assault and met his death in the baptistry, using the brace of loaded pistols Crockett or his men had placed beside his bed. In the words of Frank Dobie:

> It is generally believed that he died with bowie knife in hand, still on the cot but sitting up, back braced against the wall at his head, victims of his valor and prowess strewn around him. But it used to be claimed that at the last minute he rallied enough to stand up and meet with demoniacal fury the Mexicans coming into his room. One specifier has it that he killed two with his pistols and managed to knife into the vitals of three more before he was overwhelmed. Imagination and patriotic sympathy rebel at the idea of Bowie's dying except in the climax of hand-to-hand combat.

ONE STORY remains to be told concerning the events of March 6, 1836. By afternoon the Alamo courtyard had become silent. The smoke had thinned out against the sky; the Texan dead had been separated from the Mexicans destined for Christian burial.

Many men had died there that day—among them Daniel William Cloud from Kentucky, Micajah Autry from North Carolina, William Barret Travis from South

Carolina, Gregorio Esparza from San Antonio—but the one the young Mexican girl was looking for was not at first in sight. She went from body to body looking at the Texas fallen. In her black mantilla, a small gold cross on her breast, she was a solitary living figure among the dead.

At last she saw the body she was looking for. Kneeling down beside her lover, she folded his arms across his chest, and drawing the cross from her breast, placed it in his hands. With her handkerchief she wiped the grime of battle from his face, unshaved now for two weeks. Then, dipping it into the pool of blood at his side, she placed the handkerchief that had been first white, then gray, and was now red, between her breasts, and walked away.

There was nothing else to come but night.

News of the Alamo shook all Texas. When six weeks later the Mexican army under Santa Anna was annihilated at San Jacinto in a battle of only twenty minutes, it was cries of "Remember the Alamo" that fed the fury of the Texans. But even before this quick retribution, waves of terror and a second atrocity had shaken the country.

All Texas now seemed open for invasion. Santa Anna expected complete capitulation when news of the Alamo was learned.

The city of Gonzales was first to hear of the tragedy. The initial reaction of the town which would be the next target for Santa Anna's army was one of disbelief. When two Mexicans from San Antonio arrived on March 9 with the news, Sam Houston—who had left Washington-on-the-

Brazos on March 6 to assume command of the 350 volunteers assembled at Gonzales—ordered the newsmongers
arrested for telling lies. But he could no longer suppress
the news when Mrs. Dickinson and Travis's Joe arrived.
For twenty-four hours the little town, in which nearly
every family had a father or brother at the Alamo, was
immobilized by desolation and horror. When reaction to
stupor came, the residents began their wild escape eastward.

Houston, in an attempt to organize the chaos, stripped
his army of wagons to allow civilians to escape. As the
Gonzales residents raced eastward to the other settlements,
panic accompanied them. All Texas—save for Houston's
gradually growing new army—sped in disarray toward
the Louisiana border, abandoning farms and houses, cattle and pigs, riding mules and whatever transport could
be salvaged. In the so-called "Runaway Scrape" Santa
Anna's expectations of crumbling Texan resistance were
being fulfilled.

Meanwhile the Constitutional Convention was standing firm. So was Sam Houston, at whose insistence the
delegates remained in session. By the time they adjourned
on March 16, they had not only passed and signed a declaration of independence but had elected an ad interim government, adopted a constitution, and reappointed Houston
commander in chief of the Texan army. By then Houston
was retreating along the Brazos River from the three-
pronged Mexican advance.

His main force was still at Goliad with Colonel Fannin.
Upon learning of the fall of the Alamo he ordered Fannin
to retreat to Victoria, about thirty miles eastward and near
a Texan-held port on the Gulf. Fannin got the order on

March 13, but did not begin to execute it till March 19. He had dispatched troops from Goliad to evacuate American settlers at Refugio, near San Patricio, in the path of the advancing army of General Urrea. Urrea had already exterminated the two outposts of the Matamoros project on February 27 and on March 2, when Dr. Grant was shot.

Though Fannin's impulses were kind, the delay of his retreat from Goliad proved fatal. Finally setting out on March 19, he was trapped by Urrea's army that same afternoon on Coleto Creek. Fannin and his men fought valiantly, but they were ringed around with superior guns and outnumbered three to one. The next morning, Fannin's council voted to capitulate, believing, as Fannin did, that Urrea had promised to spare the prisoners and return them to the States. But they were kept at Goliad for a week, and then on Palm Sunday, March 27, were marched out and brutally and unsuspectingly massacred by Mexican troops. The Texans, thinking they were being marched to the Gulf, were shot down from behind while they were en route. Fannin died with dignity, asking only that he be buried and not be shot in the face. His face was ripped to shreds by gunfire and he was not buried. Santa Anna had countermanded Urrea's leniency. He meant again to terrorize the Texans into abject surrender.

What he did finally was to galvanize Texas into a mighty resistance. After Goliad, Houston retreated cannily, in opposition to the will of his officers, who wanted to strike back at once. On April 21, Santa Anna—who had rejoined his army after a three-week rest in San Antonio—wandered with almost unbelievable stupidity into a terrible trap at San Jacinto, near Galveston. Houston had merely to close the trap. So startling was the Texans' surprise attack that the battle lasted only twenty minutes.

To the *grito* of "Remember the Alamo" was added a new cry: "Remember Goliad."

"*Me no Alamo!*" yelled some of the surrendering Mexicans as six hundred of their comrades were killed in less than half an hour. It was the only major battle in American history in which none of the enemy escaped death or capture. At San Jacinto, Texas won what it had already formally declared: its recognition as an independent republic. At San Jacinto, the Texans captured the conqueror of the Alamo. But Santa Anna was released the next year and lived to fight again against the *norteamericanos*—in the war with Mexico in 1846.

Of the Alamo itself, of those who died there and those who miraculously were still alive when the tumult and smoke died down, little more remains to be said. On the Texan side 182 men, including the thirty-two from Gonzales, were killed; about fifteen women and children were spared. Jim Bowie's slave boy, Sam, was released, as was Travis's Joe, who was first treated to a course of indoctrination, shown the sight of a triumphant military parade, and freed by Santa Anna to tell the insurgent Texans the *generalissimo* could march on Washington if he chose. In this way Santa Anna hoped to frighten away volunteers to the Texas army from the States. He need not have bothered. Sam Houston's army cut him down before volunteers from the north could arrive.

Mexican casualties at the Alamo were staggering. A conservative estimate set their losses between 1,200 and 1,500 men, or ten to one for the Texan dead. The most conservative estimate came from Santa Anna himself. In his official report he states: "We lost about seventy killed and three hundred wounded, among whom are twenty-five officers." Since in the same report he refers to finding six hundred Texan corpses, his figure can hardly be taken seriously. *Alcalde* Francisco Ruiz, in charge of separating Texan bodies from Mexican, estimates the Mexican dead at 1,600—a figure more than twenty times that given by Santa Anna—and calls attention to the Tolucca battalion, of whose 830 men only 130 remained alive. Sergeant Becerra placed the losses at 2,000 dead and 300 wounded. Perhaps most conclusive is the figure given to Dr. Sutherland by Santa Anna's secretary, Ramon Martinez Caro. Caro said: "We brought to San Antonio more than 5,000 men and we lost during the siege 1,544 of the best of them. The Texans fought more like devils than men." They had fought fiercely enough, at any rate, to infuriate Santa Anna. His cook Ben, who became Sam Houston's cook after the battle of San Jacinto, said the general, returning to his headquarters with Colonel Almonte directly after the battle, had been greatly incensed when the colonel commented that "another such victory would ruin them."

To Santa Anna, the Alamo *had* to be a victory, an example for all time to any Anglo-Americans who thought they might take Texas away from Mexico. Too many Americans—Travis and Houston among them—had boasted that with an army of five hundred they could march right into the halls of Montezuma and take immediate possession. It was as a vital victory, therefore, that the Alamo was entered in Santa Anna's official report. The assault began, he said, at 5 A.M. and was over by 8 A.M. Stubborn resistance was met, the heavy combat lasting an hour and a half, but valiantly overcome. His men, he says, "fought individually, vying with each other in heroism.... Twenty-one pieces of artillery, used by the enemy with the most perfect accuracy, the brisk fire of musketry, which illuminated the interior of the Fortress and its walls and ditches, could not check our dauntless soldiers."

It was a victory, and Santa Anna took the Texan flag to prove it. Flying above the west wall of the chapel, still undamaged by gunfire, it was taken after the last man had fallen and sent to Mexico City to the Secretary of War with the message: "The bearer takes with him one of the flags of the enemy's battalions, captured today. The inspection of it will show plainly the true intention of the treacherous colonists and of their abettors, who came from the ports of the United States of the North." The message apparently referred to the numerals "1824," a reminder of the now-invalidated constitution.

The Mexicans seized other than just flags. They took almost everything they could lay hands on. One of the more interesting objects was Davy Crockett's diary, which was found, allegedly, in General Castrillon's trunk at San Jacinto.

But looting was slight consolation for the loss of 1,500 men. So heavy were the Mexican losses, Ruiz reports, that the graveyard could not hold them all and a number of Mexican dead had to be thrown into the river. The choked current could not carry all the corpses away, and when the buzzards came, with the stench growing intolerable, it is said that Santa Anna himself fell ill of it.

One reason for the staggering number of Mexican dead may lie in Santa Anna's indifference to medical care for his wounded. Dr. John Barnard, who was captured at Goliad and sent to San Antonio at Ugartechea's urgent demand for somebody who could "amputate limbs," reported, six weeks after the fall, that there were still 100 wounded there, desperately in need of help. "I see many around the town who were crippled then, *apparently two or three hundred,* and the citizens tell me three or four hundred have died of their wounds. . . . Their surgical department is shockingly conducted—not an amputation performed before we arrived, although there are several cases even now that should have been operated on at the first, and how many have died of the want of operation it is impossible to tell. . . . There has been scarcely a ball cut out as yet, every patient carrying the lead that he received that morning. . . ."

The prisoners taken by Santa Anna received—surprisingly—better treatment. At the Músquiz house where the women and children had been taken, Santa Anna doled out his mercy, assigning to each woman a blanket and two silver dollars.

None had a stranger tale to tell than Mrs. Dickinson. Santa Anna, always a man of caprice, wanted to adopt her daughter.

While still under guard in the Alamo, Mrs. Dickinson heard an approaching Mexican officer ask, in English, "Is there a Mrs. Dickinson here?" She had been afraid to answer, until he added, "If you value your life, speak up." She identified herself, and some of the soldiers started to seize her, misunderstanding the officer's intent. "Leave her alone," he told them, "the general has need of her."

As she went out by the courtyard, her daughter Angelina Arabella in her arms, a stray shot hit her in the calf of her right leg. The severe wound required her to be carried, but it was treated and she was made comfortable as soon as the escort reached the Músquiz house.

There her interview with Santa Anna must have completed her agonized bewilderment on this tragic day. He admired her baby endlessly, could not stop considering it. Like many another cruel man, he was sentimental about children. Now that Mrs. Dickinson was husbandless, he pointed out, and the child fatherless, the baby needed protection. Santa Anna offered himself. If the child came with him, she would have all that money could buy, security, a splendid future. Mrs. Dickinson, though grateful for having her life saved, was rendered speechless by this proposition. Santa Anna persisted, no doubt inviting the mother to come along too. According to her granddaughter, Mrs. Dickinson finally was able to gasp that she could never consider letting her child belong to a man who had killed its father. Santa Anna's sensitivity was stung and he persisted no more.

It was through the intervention of her friend Mrs. Ramón Músquiz, Mrs. Dickinson always believed, that Santa Anna had first learned of her and her plight. Wrapping around her Captain Dickinson's Masonic apron (Santa Anna was a York Rite Mason), Mrs. Músquiz had gone in person to plead with Santa Anna to save her friend. Only after long hesitation did the dictator agree; then he went further suddenly decreeing that no woman or child in the fortress should be harmed.

Oddly enough, Santa Anna got his adopted American child, but years later, after he had returned to Mexico following the battle of San Jacinto. It was a twelve-year-old boy named John Christopher Columbus Hill, who had insisted upon accompanying his father and brother on a foolhardy Texas expedition to the little town of Mier.

When the Texas army was captured and lined up to hand over their guns, young Hill jumped out of line and smashed his gun over a rock. General Ampudia, leading the

Mexicans, had just the day before lost his son in the battle. He said to the lad sadly: "My *hijito*, my little man, what are you doing so far away from your mother?"

The boy explained that he had sworn to his family never to give up his gun. He had shot ten Mexican soldiers with it, he said.

So impressed was Ampudia with this show of valor that he kept the boy beside him, taught him Spanish, and sent him to Santa Anna in the capital. The shrewd general offered a trade to the lad. He would liberate the boy's father and brother if John Hill would live in Mexico and train for a military career at the Army School. Young Hill was shrewd too. He would not train to lead Mexican troops against Anglo-Americans, he said, but he would train as an engineer.

Santa Anna accepted. He cherished the boy as though he were his own, and John Christopher Columbus Hill had a long and distinguished life and career in Mexico. But ironically his Mexican hero was never Santa Anna. It was Benito Juarez.

THERE REMAINED now on March 6 at the Alamo only the matter of burning the enemy dead. By three o'clock in the afternoon the bodies had been sorted and the fires made ready. *Alcalde* Ruiz of San Antonio had been in charge of bringing in wood and dry branches from the "neighboring forests," and had supervised the laying down of the alternating layers of wood and dry twigs and bodies of the fallen. There were three or four stacks, rising several layers high. Grease and oil had been used to soak the bodies.

The tradition of burning the enemy dead was an old one, going back to Homer's heroes at Troy and beyond. In carrying it out now Santa Anna was not merely reliving the cruelty he had learned from General Arredondo twenty-three years before. He was giving an example to all revolutionaries in North America and throughout the world of what would happen to those who followed their "manifest destiny."

The example was made, but not in the way Santa Anna intended it. Travis, Bowie, Crockett, Bonham, and the others were to become supreme examples throughout the world of how a man can live on by dying. In the words of Frank Dobie, the men crossing Travis's line had the choice between life and immortality. Perhaps it is history's lesson that they chose well.

Now, as the torch was applied and the flames rose, their names were being carried to Gonzales, to Goliad, to San Jacinto. Fourteen of the burning dead, it is said, were unknown soldiers, unidentified, unmourned, unsung, lost. But the name "Alamo" was not. It became a battle cry that brought to defeat the men who thought they had defeated it.

In the late afternoon sky the flames rose and disappeared. The wind was rising. The Alamo that began in defeat ended in resurrection.

Notes

Chapter 1: THE FIRST DAY

Page 1. The placing of Daniel Cloud in the bell tower is the author's single assumption in this book as to the position of any character at any specific time; elsewhere all movement of participants is based on documentary evidence. Cloud himself is known from his letters to his family; the presence of the sentry is testified to in many accounts.

Page 19. Ambrosio Rodriguez was a descendant of Canary Islanders who came to San Antonio in 1731. The memoirs of his son J. R. Rodriguez have been preserved.

Page 23, line 18. Austin's attitude toward annexation changed gradually from his early position of forbearance. On November 22 he wrote his nephew: "We ought to get united to the U.S. as soon as possible. It is the best we can do." On January 7, two weeks after setting off with Branch T. Archer and William H. Wharton as commissioners to the United States to enlist aid and sympathy, he wrote back: "I advise you to take an open and bold stand for independence at once."

The commissioners made slow progress on their mission. Detained by snow and ice, they did not reach Washington, D.C., until March 30. So chaotic were things in Texas that they received little word of the happenings there.

Chapter 2: SUTHERLAND AND SMITH

Page 41. In his memoirs, Santa Anna claims he could have quickly vanquished the Texans on the morning of February 23 if his cavalry had not failed to execute the surprise attack he had ordered. It seems reasonable that Cloud's bell ringing and the sight of scouts Sutherland and Smith prevented the surprise.

Chapter 3: THE MISSION

Page 53. A legendary account has it that Santa Anna arrived in San Antonio in time to attend, disguised, the fandango in honor of George Washington's birthday.

The rumor could possibly be confused with the report of Antonio Menchaca, a Mexican resident of San Antonio, that at the earlier fandango of February 11, celebrating the arrival of Davy Crockett from Tennessee, a messenger arrived from the border with an important note for Menchaca, known to be a friend of Jim Bowie. The message verified that Santa Anna reached the Rio Grande in early February, and stated erroneously that he had 13,000 men.

Since both Bowie and Travis read Spanish, Menchaca signaled to them. Bowie came at once, but Travis continued dancing. When Bowie approached to say that he had significant war news, Travis replied: "Not now, I am occupied with the most beautiful señorita in San Antonio." Travis, at last reading the note, reflected a moment and then reckoned that it would take Santa Anna ten or twelve days to reach San Antonio. It took, in reality, exactly ten.

The other legend has it that Santa Anna, frustrated in his plans of surprise attack, attended the George Washington Birthday celebration dressed as a civilian. Here he estimated enemy strength, perhaps gazed on the beauty Travis was dancing with, and slipped away after being recognized by some of the Mexicans. While the story would account for the Mexican exodus on the morning of February 23, it contains too many coincidental elements to be believed.

Page 55. The ill-fated revolution of 1813 was only one of the splinter revolts initiated by the priest Hidalgo and organized by his disciple Bernardo Gutierrez to secure Mexico's independence from Spain. Santa Anna, who first fought against the movement, moved to the winning side after its triumph in 1821.

Page 57. Santa Anna's pride was his most outstanding characteristic. His aide, General Filisola, refers often to the generalissimo's "vanity." Filisola, it should be noted, was critical of Santa Anna's handling of the entire assault.

Chapter 4: SIEGE

Page 58. Enrique Esparza reported these details years later in newspaper interviews.

Page 61, line 13. Bowie's note, preserved in Mexican archives, says specifically that Jameson is being sent under cover of truce "to ascertain if it be true that a parley was called" by the Mexican side.

Page 66, line 4. Travis's entries are still to be seen, in his own handwriting, in the Travis Family Bible in the Archives of the State of Texas.

Page 67. The oral tradition of Travis's reasons for leaving his wife are documented in Ruby Mixon's thesis, "William Barret Travis" (University of Texas). In addition to persons quoted as sources there, Miss Mixon gave me in an interview what may be regarded as later trustworthy confirmation. Fire destroyed Conecuh County Court House and its records in 1833.

Chapter 5: THE SECOND DAY: BOWIE

Page 75, line 21. As late as 1841 Rezin Bowie was still buying and selling ancient Spanish land grants.

Page 79, line 14. The cholera epidemic nearly wrecked Austin's colony in Texas, taking off a number of the most useful citizens. Austin himself had a bout with it in Mexico City, where in 1833 it took a toll of ten thousand lives in the Mexican capital alone.

Page 79, line 30. Navarro's letter continues: "I have lost a loyal brother-in-law in Veramendi, and Texas a good son, a faithful and interested friend. Texas is now a political orphan in the government of the state."

Page 80, line 22. Jim Bowie's speech at the Texas Consultation of 1835 is very revealing of his character. He failed to get what he obviously wanted: to be named commander-in-chief of the Texas army. Travis and Governor Smith, now punctuating their speeches and letters with appeals to "white superiority," distrusted Bowie as a Mexican citizen.

Page 82, line 19. McNeill made this report as a witness in one of the law cases concerning Bowie's estate.

Page 82, line 27. The holdings of John T. Mason's New York Company, of which Bowie was deputy administrator, dwarf the present largest holding in Texas, the ¾-million-acre King Ranch. In possibly thinking of his own holdings while disobeying his orders to destroy the Alamo, Bowie revealed how realistic his mind really was.

Page 84, line 25. Travis and Bowie were both bitter about Austin's failure to recognize them. To the patient, gentle Austin, they were types to be feared: Travis as a firebrand who had already involved Texas in unnecessary action; Bowie as a land-hungry speculator with too great a reputation for killing men.

Page 87, line 3. It is interesting to note that Travis does not mention Bowie again in his correspondence after this critical report.

Chapter 6: WILLIAM B. TRAVIS

Page 93. The Travis Diary opens on August 31, 1833, and closes on June 25, 1834. It remained for another year and a half in Travis's office at San Felipe, and was brought away by his partner F. J. Starr "at the burning of San Felipe by the order of Genl Houston in 1836." Travis noted in his diary that he had written in 1833 a complete summary of his life up to that time, but this paper has not been found. Whether

Travis continued the practice of keeping a diary after going to the Alamo can never be known.

Page 96, line 3. Rebecca Cummins is sometimes confused with Mary Elizabeth Cummins. The two girls were not related.

Page 96, line 13. The entire record for August 31, when Travis apparently met Rebecca Cummins, is as follows:

> "Rose early—got lost [Travis was returning to San Felipe]—took breakfast at Stevenson's—Bobbitt will be down to San Felipe with his note at the last of the week—Got mule fed at Edward's—paid 25—dined at Cummins paid 25—arrived at San Felipe—Took supper at Jones'—lost at monte 15.62½—borrowed of Cisto $5.00."

Page 98, line 22. One of the most tantalizing entries in the diary is the one of January 2, 1834, reading "Duel &—."

Chapter 7: SANTA ANNA

Page 103. The precise date of Santa Anna's mock marriage is not known, but it is not unreasonable to assume it occurred the second day of the siege. The story is documented in many Mexican sources.

Page 106, line 20. Santa Anna's remark to Colonel Minon, "I shall send her to Mexico and save her for my old age," was partly prophetic. The general's carriage did leave shortly for San Luis Potosi on a mission which General Filisola in his *Memoirs* attributed to a "scandal." The girl bore Santa Anna a baby in San Luis Potosi.

This episode, reported by Sergeant Juan Becerra of the Mexican army, is corroborated by General Filisola and Santa Anna's secretary, Ramon Martinez Caro.

Page 109, line 4. Pollard had written Governor Smith ten days before the siege: "I wish General Houston was now on the frontier to help us crush both our external and internal enemies—let us show them how republicans can and will fight."

Chapter 8: DAYS OF HOPE: CROCKETT

Page 118, line 30. Santa Anna's movements here are based on the diary of his aide, Colonel Almonte.

Chapter 9: JIM BONHAM

Page 147, line 16. Bonham is still uniformly called "Colonel Bonham" in Texas. Pronounced "Bone-em" by the family, but Texans call it "Bahn-em."

Chapter 10: COLONEL JAMES W. FANNIN

The best source: Clarence Wharton's *Remember Goliad.*

Chapter 11: THE NINTH DAY: GONZALES

Pages 163, line 18. Green DeWitt, most famous of the empresarios after Stephen F. Austin, died in Monclova while representing Texas at the state legislature.

Chapter 12: "ONE OF THE MOST PATHETIC DAYS IN TIME"

Page 171, line 8. Dilue Harris in her diary reports how she and other children melted lead to make bullets for the insurgent Texans.

Page 172, line 18. The Texas force meeting General Urrea near San Patricio had practically defied restraining orders from Sam Houston.

Page 177, line 7. Tradition in San Antonio, where John W. Smith later served as mayor, has it that he escaped through secret underground tunnels connecting the five old San Antonio missions. No recent excavation has verified the existence of such tunnels.

His descendants add another interesting legend—that he was nearly apprehended at one point but escaped capture by hiding under the skirts of a Mexican woman doing her washing in the irrigation ditch. According to this story, he found a horse in town and rode it to the Texas convention. Since he obviously had his horse with him after piloting in the thirty-two Gonzales men, this story cannot be believed.

Page 185. The Rose episode, whatever argument may attend it, has lodged in the public mind to become part of the Alamo record as it is remembered and told. In justice to Rose, it must be pointed out that he had not shared the American frontier experience so meaningful to the others and that he had already seen his share of suffering in the Moscow campaign.

Page 190, line 12. This story is reported by Mrs. Holley. It is in manuscript, in diary form, at the Archives Division of the Eugene C. Barker History Center of the University of Texas.

Chapter 13: THE LAST DAY

Page 198, line 8. The time of the attack is indicated in a quatrain of unknown origin composed not long after the Alamo fell:

> It was on one Domingo morning,
> Just at the break of day,
> That holy Sabbath morning
> When Christians went to pray.

Page 198, line 16. Ben reported later that the illumination of the Texan eighteen-pounder gave him a clear view of the battle.

Page 210, line 15. The report of Anselmo Borgarra and Antonio Perez to Sam Houston concerning Travis's death was widely believed in 1836 but has been nearly forgotten since.

Page 211, line 12. W. F. Gray, the distinguished Virginian, passing through the state, was very much impressed with Joe's modesty and clear presentation in his report. Joe's story is the one followed in most subsequent chronicles of the Alamo.

Page 213, line 31. The following note, from Edith S. Halter, curator of the Alamo, throws an interesting light on Davy's gun:

> "After many years of searching for the whereabouts of David Crockett's famous 'Old Betsy,' it was a joy finally to locate it in Little Rock, Arkansas. This gun had been presented to Crockett by the young men of Philadelphia, and at that time Crockett said it was the most beautiful gun he had ever seen. Some of the Crockett descendants have told me he called it his 'beautiful Betsy.'
>
> "I felt sure that the gun would be marked in a way that could identify it. On June 30, 1955, I had a reply from my letter to Mrs. J. W. Crockett, widow of a great-grandson of David. She stated that the gun was in the Treasury vault at Little Rock. Though the gun belongs to her daughter, Mrs. A. S. Holderness, it is being kept in the vault for safety.
>
> "The inscription down the length of the barrel reads 'Presented by the young men of Philadelphia to the Honorable David Crockett.' Just behind the sign at the end of the barrel is 'Go ahead.' "

Page 221, line 10. Caro's account is told in his *Verdadera Idea.*

Page 223, line 6. When the Texas army gathered to storm Béxar under Stephen F. Austin, it was Almeron Dickinson who made the carriage for their single cannon, the one salvaged from Ugartechea at Gonzales.

Page 224, line 16. As late as 1956 an American popular magazine was claiming to have found new evidence of Crockett's escape in Mexican files. The exact source was not divulged. In his official report, Santa Anna specifically mentions seeing "cadavers" of "Buy," "Travis," and "Crocket."

Page 225, line 5. Walter Worthington Bowie in his history of the family says that Bowie died in a delirium only an hour or so before the attack. Dr. Sutherland, on the other hand, claims to have seen two years after the battle the blood stains on the wall where Bowie's brains had been spattered. He carefully interviewed Travis's boy Joe, he says, who confirmed what Mrs. Dickinson had told the doctor: "Several balls went through Bowie's head while he lay unable to lift it from his pillow."

The story about Bowie's eloquent defense of liberty was told by a fifer in the Mexican army to W. P. Zuber. According to this account, Bowie was found late in the afternoon, still alive. Four soldiers brought him to their captain, where preparations for the burning of the bodies were already being made. The captain, knowing of Bowie's Mexican citizenship, accused him of treason. Bowie replied that it was the Mexicans fighting to uphold Santa Anna's destruction of the constitution who were the traitors. The captain, infuriated, ordered his men to spread-eagle Bowie and cut out his tongue. When the body was tossed on the funeral pyre, the flames were said to have shot to majestic heights.

The story is typical of the legends surrounding Bowie's death.

Page 225, line 23. Madam Candelaria's accounts, given in her old age, were self-contradictory and there is strong reason to believe she was not in the Alamo. Though her relationship to Bowie was not clearly defined, the Texas government awarded her bounties given to families of the defenders of the Alamo.

EPILOGUE

Page 231, line 18. The evidence of Santa Anna's Ben and Travis's Joe is integral to all reconstructions of the events of the Alamo. Ben, who had made a great reputation in Washington (and, later, on steamboats in the Gulf) as an expert chef, was captured at San Jacinto and made Sam Houston's cook. It was Ben who accompanied Santa Anna when the Generalissimo asked to see the bodies of the Texas leaders. Ben's testimony is largely supported by that of Joe, who owed his life to Colonel Barragan when two Mexican soldiers, seeing him with a gun, assumed he had fired it and were ready to shoot him down. He was saved and later freed to warn the Texans of Mexican military might. Oddly enough, not a single word of testimony has survived from Bowie's servant, Sam.

Page 231, line 30. Santa Anna stated: "More than six hundred corpses of foreigners were buried in the ditches and entrenchments and a great many who had escaped the bayonet of the infantry fell in the vicinity under the sabres of the cavalry." Since less than two hundred Texans were in the Alamo and the Texan bodies were burned rather than buried, one can only assume he is exaggerating for the benefit of citizens at home. Alcalde Francisco Ruiz, whose testimony is unquestioned, states: "The men [Texans] burned were one hundred and eighty-two. I was an eye-witness, for as Alcalde of San Antonio, I was with some of the neighbors, collecting the dead bodies and placing them on the funeral pyre."

Page 232, line 2. Ruiz's figure of 1,600 Mexican dead was the one carried to Gonzales by Mrs. Dickinson and Travis's Joe. The leading Texas newspaper of the day, Gail Borden's *Telegraph and Texas Register,* on March 24 reckoned the combined dead and wounded list for the enemy at about 1,500. The Navarro family in San Antonio sent this figure to Juan Seguin at Gonzales. Other Mexican citizens in San Antonio estimated the dead at about 1,000. Other reports include those of Ben, Jesse Badgett of Houston's staff, the cautious estimate of Captain Potter, and the report of Dr. Sutherland after his interview with Ramon Martinez Caro. The last-named is probably most conclusive. Both Santa Anna and Almonte were present at the interview, Sutherland notes, and neither of them contradicted Caro's statement.

Page 234, line 10. Dr. Barnard's report goes on to say:

> "Yesterday and today we have been around with the surgeons of the place to visit the wounded, and a pretty piece of work 'Travis and his faithful few' have made of them. There are now about 100 of the wounded here. The surgeons tell us that 400 of them were brought into the hospital the morning they stormed the Alamo but I think from appearances there must have been many more than that number."

He also tells of receiving an urgent request to care for the wife of the head surgeon of the garrison:

> "On going to the house to see her, I found that she merely had the toothache. This man amputated the leg of one of the wounded men on the day that we arrived. The man died next day. We have amputated but one limb, and the man is doing well. A dozen more need this service, but they will die anyway, so there is no need to do it."

Page 235, line 17. Mrs. Dickinson thought Mrs. Músquiz's attitude was typical of the Mexican citizenry of San Antonio, who were at once appalled and saddened when they learned of Santa's Anna's determination to exterminate the men in the fortress without mercy. This hardly tallies with the attitude described by Travis in his last letter to Governor Smith. It should be noted, however, that both Travis and Smith had little sympathy for the Mexican position.

Page 235, line 22. The character of Mrs. Alsbury, daughter of Angel Navarro and sister-in-law to Jim Bowie, is an interesting one and reflects the suspicion cast upon Mexican citizens by the Anglo-American population. General Filisola in his memoirs reports (as a rumor) that Travis sent a Mexican lady from the Alamo on March 4 with an offer of truce. Mrs. Dickinson claimed that the woman was Mrs. Horace Alsbury, and that she had gone, not representing Travis, but as a spy to betray to Santa Anna the weakening condition of the men in the Alamo. This knowledge, Mrs. Dickinson held, enabled the dictator to select the right day for the attack.

Another report says that her father, Angel Navarro, got permission from Santa Anna to carry away his two daughters (Mrs. Alsbury and her sister Gertrudis) before the assault began.

The evidence confirms neither of these accounts. Mrs. Alsbury claimed she was nursing Jim Bowie the day the Alamo fell. When she and her sister sought shelter in a side room, a Mexican soldier grabbed Gertrudis Navarro and tore the shawl from her shoulders. A sick Texan, trying to defend her, was bayoneted. Enrique Esparza confirms much of this, stating that she was in the chapel until the very end. He also remembered seeing her at the Músquiz house later with the other prisoners. Mrs. Dickinson's story may be discredited as an example of anti-Mexican sentiment, entirely understandable on her part.

Page 237. No one knows with any certainty what happened to the ashes or bones of the burned Texan bodies, though a number of divergent claims have been made. Adina de Zavala says one pyre burned in the Alamo courtyard and three others outside the walls. It was a year later, on February 25, 1837, before the new Texas Republic remembered to give a Christian burial to the relicts of the Alamo men. Sam Houston ordered Captain Juan Seguin, then in command of the Béxar post, to collect what relicts he could find. Although Dr. Sutherland held that the ceremony was a hoax, Seguin, writing forty-four years later, tells how he "collected the fragments, placed them in an urn and buried it in the Cathedral of San Fernando, immediately in front of the altar—that is, in front of the railing and near the steps." It seems unlikely, however, that any bones would have remained a year later, with wild dogs roaming the prairie, and equally unlikely that the pious Mexicans would have allowed to be buried in the Cathedral the bones of 183 men they considered to be heretics and rebels.

J. M. Rodriguez, on the other hand, claims that the ashes were buried reverently shortly after the pyres stopped smoking. And Dr. Sutherland states that a company of Rangers, shortly after the battle of San Jacinto, visited the Alamo and buried the ashes of its defenders in "a peach orchard" in the shadow of the mission where they fell. The exact place is unimportant. It is as a symbol, rather than as a monument, that the Alamo is imperishable.

Principal Sources

Accounts of the Alamo began appearing in print soon after the battle. The January, February, March and April, 1836, issues of *El Mosquito Mexicano* carried eyewitness Mexican accounts, and the *Telegraph and Texas Register* carried news of the battle as it was learned, as well as a partial list of the Texan dead. The news was spread throughout the United States in April by reprintings of Sam Houston's letter to Fannin of March 11.

Systematic treatments of the fall had to wait until much later. The earliest was that of Capt. Reuben Marmaduke Potter, printed in the *Texas Almanac* in 1868. Captain Potter was living in Matamoros when the Alamo fell; he later talked with many Mexican soldiers about the battle and, two years after the fall, studied the Alamo siege under the guidance of Capt. Juan Seguin. Potter continued to revise and elaborate his account. The 1904 version in the *Magazine of American History* is no doubt the most authoritative source originating from a reporter alive at the time of the tragedy.

A number of Texans left accounts, of which the most useful are those of Dr. John Sutherland, J. M. Rodriguez (*Memoirs*, 1913), and Antonio Menchaca (*Memoirs*, first published in English translation by San Antonio's Yanaguana Society in 1937). Rodriguez and Menchaca were Mexicans of San Antonio friendly to the Texas cause; Sutherland's account has the virtue of immediacy, in his actually being in the Alamo until sent out by Travis. Other Texans who left records were Col. John Ford, Noah Smithwick, James Field, Gov. Frank Lubbock, Capt. John Duval, John Swisher, and others. The files of the *Southwestern Historical Quarterly* are extremely rich in early Texas material.

For all this, it must be admitted that the historical material about the Alamo is disappointingly slight. As James Atkins Shackford observes in his *David Crockett* (1956): "I suppose no event in recent historical times, with a basis in fact, has been more conducive to the creation of legend, fiction, gossip, error and falsehood than the destruction of the fortress at San Antonio de Bexar . . . Except for the date and the fact of its fall, there is almost no single point about the Alamo upon which the testimony of the few survivors does not disagree." The few Texan survivors—women and children and two Negro slave boys—were in hiding or understandably overcome with fear. The only reliable witnesses to the battle itself—those on the Mexican side—produced their accounts, as Dr. Carlos Castaneda has demonstrated in his *The Mexican Side of the Texas Revolution*, after the defeat at San Jacinto, when their impulse was to shift blame for the defeat.

Even so, two of the most interesting contributions to Alamo investigation in recent years are Mexican items: The private diary of Col. Gonzales Pena (who fought at the Alamo), privately printed in Mexico City in 1956 by Frank de Sanchez; and the discovery in 1936 of a private record kept inside ledger books by Maurice Sanchez during his years as a Mexican border official at Matamoros (1833–1849), a summation of the latter appearing in the Summer, 1951, issue of the *Texas Library Journal.* Both these items, like two recent biographies of Santa Anna and Vasconcelo's new history of Mexico, follow the vitriolic pattern of the memoirs of General Santa Anna and of his secretary, Ramon Martinez Caro. More objective is the two-volume memoir of General Vicente Filisola, first appearing in 1848 and somewhat revised in 1849.

Because of the dearth of reliable material, I have been fortunate in being preceded by two monumental works of scholarship. Amelia Williams's "A Critical Study of the Siege of the Alamo," written in 1931 as a doctoral dissertation at the University of Texas and printed in part in Volumes XXXVI (1932–1933) and XXXVII (1933–1934) of the *Southwestern Historical Quarterly,* was the first great work of productive scholarship on the Alamo, and is still the best of its kind. Beside this must be placed the brilliant 400-page thesis of Ruby Mixon, "William Barret Travis," also in manuscript form at the University of Texas.

In addition, I have been fortunate in being supplied certain materials by descendants of Alamo families. Mrs. J. Leonard Smith of Dallas supplied me with information on William Barret Travis; Mrs. William Campbell of San Antonio and her aunt, Mrs. Frank C. Gillespie, furnished scrapbooks concerning their ancestor, John C. Smith, and related a number of anecdotes that have remained in the family tradition. The story of John Christopher Columbus Hill in Chapter 13 was given me by Miss Nina Hill of Austin. Manuscripts in the Eugene C. Barker Center at Austin, the Texas State Library, the Texas State Archives, the Texas collection of the *Dallas News,* and the Wagner collection of Southwestern materials at Yale University also yielded items.

Among the significant present-day materials should be listed J. Frank Dobie's "James Bowie: Big Dealer," first printed in the January, 1957, issue of the *Southwestern Historical Quarterly;* the two-volume *Handbook of Texas,* prepared under the direction of Walter Prescott Webb and Bailey Carroll; and Wortham's five-volume *History of Texas,* particularly good on the Texas revolution. Paul Horgan's *Great River: The Rio Grande in North American History* is a brilliant study of the history of the entire Southwest.

The most recent modern telling of the Alamo story is John Myers Myers's *The Alamo* (1947), told with great skill and humor. Only the latter fifth of the book is devoted to the siege.

A selective list of books I have found most profitable follows.

MANUSCRIPTS

The Travis Diary, 1833–1834 (Eugene C. Barker Texas History Center, University of Texas)

Ruby Mixon, "William Barret Travis" (thesis, University of Texas)

Amelia Williams, "The Siege and Fall of the Alamo" (doctoral dissertation, University of Texas. NOTE: Published, but not in entirety, in *Southwestern Historical Quarterly*, 1932–1934)

H. A. McArdle, "The Alamo Book" (Texas State Archives, Austin)

Asbury Papers (Barker Center, University of Texas)

Fontaine Papers (Barker Center, University of Texas)

John S. Ford's Journal (Texas State Archives)

Blake Papers (Barker Center, University of Texas)

Letters of John C. Smith, Christopher Columbus Hill, Travis family memoranda, Bowie estate legal investigations in the possession, respectively, of Mrs. Frank Gillespie (San Antonio), Miss Nina Hill (Austin), Mrs. J. Leonard Smith (Dallas), and J. Frank Dobie (Austin)

Army Papers, Texas State Library

NEWSPAPERS

El Mosquito Mexicano: 1/22; 2/5; 3/4; 4/5–1836

Telegraph and Texas Register, 1835–1836

Files of the *San Antonio Express*

Files of the *San Antonio Light*

Files of the *Dallas Morning News* (which first published the earliest contemporary studies: those of Capt. Reuben Marmaduke Potter (in the *News'* Texas Almanac of 1868) and of Dr. John Sutherland, and W. P. Zuber's account of Moses Rose's escape)

BIOGRAPHIES

Eugene C. Barker, *The Life of Stephen F. Austin;* Llerena Friend, *Sam Houston: The Great Designer;* Marquis James, *The Raven;* J. Frank Dobie, "James Bowie: Big Dealer" (privately printed monograph); Herbert Gambrell, *Anson Jones: The Last President of Texas;* Wilfrid Hardy Callcott, *Santa Anna;* Frank C. Hanighen, *Santa Anna;* Fuentes Mares, *Santa Anna: Aurora y Ocaso de un Comediante;* Walter McCaleb, *William Barret Travis;* James Atkins Shackford, *David Crockett;* Jack C. Butterfield, *Men of the Alamo, Goliad and San Jacinto;* Claude Leroy Douglas, *James Bowie;* Constance Rourke, *Davy Crockett;* Andrew Jackson Sowell, *Rangers and Pioneers of Texas;* José Valades, *Santa Anna y la Guerra de Tejas;* Clarence R. Wharton, *El Presidente* (life of Santa Anna, in English); Raymond W. Thorp, *Bowie Knife.*

CONTEMPORARY ACCOUNTS

Vicente Filisola, *La Guerra de Tejas;* Carlos Castañeda, *The Mexican Side of the Texas Revolution* (includes excerpts from memoirs and diaries of Santa Anna, Filisola, Caro, Urrea, and Tornel); Antonio Menchaca, *Memoirs;* J. M. Rodrigues, *Memoirs;* J. Sanchez Garza, *La Rebelión de Texas* (comprising annotated memoirs of a participant at the Alamo under Santa Anna, Col. Gonzalez Peña); John Sutherland, *The Fall of the Alamo;* John S. Ford, *Origin and Fall of the Alamo;* Reuben Marmaduke Potter, *The Fall of the Alamo;* Dr. John H. Barnard, *Journal;* John Milton Swisher, *Journal;* Juan N. Almonte, *Journal;* David Crockett, *A Narrative of the Life of David Crockett, Written by Himself;* Joseph Field, *Three Years in Texas;* Noah Smithwick, *Evolution of a State;* Frank R. Lubbock, *Recollections of a Governor;* John C. Duval, *Early Times in Texas;* William F. Gray, *From Virginia to Texas;* Hermann Ehrenberg, *Fahrten und Schicksale Eines Deutschen in Texas;* Frank Templeton, *Margaret Ballentine, Or, The Fall of the Alamo;* Mirabeau Bonaparte Lamar, *The Papers of Mirabeau Bonaparte Lamar;* Chester Newell, *History of the Revolution in Texas;* Eugene C. Barker, *The Austin Papers;* Mme. Calderon de la Barca, *Life in Mexico;* William Bollaert, *William Bollaert's Texas;* John J. Linn, *Reminiscences of Fifty Years in Texas.*

SPECIAL STUDIES OF THE ALAMO, SAN ANTONIO, AND THE TEXAN REVOLUTION

John Myers Myers, *The Alamo;* Albert Curtis, *Fabulous San Antonio;* Adina de Zavala, *The Alamo;* Frederick C. Chabot, *The Alamo—As Shrine, Mission and Fortress;* Frederick C. Chabot, *With the Makers of San Antonio;* William C. Corner, *San Antonio;* William H. Brooker, *Texas: A Souvenir;* A. Garland Adair and M. H. Crockett, Sr., *Heroes of the Alamo;* A. Frances Scarborough, *Stories from the History of Texas;* Juan Agustin Morfi, *History of Texas;* Andrew Jackson Houston, *Texas Independence;* James T. DeShields, *Tall Men with Long Rifles;* Amelia Williams, "A Critical Study of the Siege of the Alamo" (*Southwestern Historical Quarterly,* 1932–1934); D. C. Baker, *A Texas Scrapbook;* (See also above "Contemporary Accounts" and Carlos Castañeda, *The Mexican Side of the Texas Revolution*); Clarence Wharton, *Remember Goliad,* W. C. Binkley, *The Texas Revolution;* Sam and Bess Woolford, *The San Antonio Story;* Rena Maverick Green, *Samuel Maverick: Texan;* Charles M. Barnes, *Combats and Conquests of Immortal Heroes.*

HISTORIES OF TEXAS (NOTE: title not listed if "History of Texas")

Hubert Howe Bancroft, *History of the North Mexican States and Texas;* Herbert E. Bolton, *With the Makers of Texas;* John Henry Brown; Carlos Castañeda, *Our Catholic Heritage in Texas* (7 vols.); Henry Stuart Foote; Francis White Johnson (edited by Eugene C. Barker); William Kennedy; N. Doran Maillard; Lewis W. Newton and Herbert Gambrell; J. M. Morphis; Edward Stiff; Ralph W. Steen, *The Texas News;* Frank Goodwyn, *Lone Star Land;* Homer Thrall, *A Pictorial History of Texas;* Dudley Goodall Wooten; Peter Molyneaux; Henderson Yoakum; George Sessions Perry, *Texas: A World in Itself;* Sam Acheson, *35,000 Days in Texas;* Louis J. Wortham.

HISTORIES OF MEXICO

Bancroft (see above); José Vasconcelos, *Breve Historia de Mexico;* Carlos Pereyra, *Tejas: La Primera Desmembración de Méjico;* Alessio Robles, *Coahuila y Texas en la época colonial;* Vito Alessio Robles, *Coahuila y Texas desde la consumación de la Independencia hasta el Tratado de Paz de Guadalupe Hidalgo;* Lucas Alamán, *Historia de México;* Paul Horgan, *Great River: The Rio Grande in North American History;* George Lockhart Rives, *The United States and Mexico;* J. H. Schlarman, *Mexico;* Henry Bamford Parkes, *A History of Mexico;* Hudson Strode, *Timeless Mexico;* John A. Crow, *Mexico Today;* J. Fred Rippy, *The United States and Mexico.*

MISCELLANEOUS

Walter Prescott Webb and H. Bailey Carroll, editors, *The Handbook of Texas;* files of the *Texas Historical Quarterly* and the *Southwestern Historical Quarterly;* files of the *Southwest Review;* WPA "Texas Guide"; WPA "San Antonio City Guide"; Publications of the Texas Folk Lore Society (particularly "From Hell to Breakfast," 1944, and "In the Shadow of History," 1939); Summer 1951 issue of *The Library Chronicle of the University of Texas* (Vol. IV, No. 2); Thomas Streeter, *Bibliography of Texas.*

An Alamo Calendar, 1835–1836

ton commander of the regular army to be recruited, leaving volunteer army besieging Béxar under its own elected chief.

November 14   After deciding to defend the liberal Mexican Constitution of 1824 instead of openly declaring independence, the Consultation adjourns to meet again at Washington-on-the-Brazos March 1, 1836.

November 24   Austin leaves volunteer army to accept role as emissary to the United States to get volunteers and guns and money. Burleson elected to succeed him; Francis Johnson next in command.

December 5   Exiled Mexican leaders—Lorenzo de Zavala and General Mexía (working with former vice-president Gomez Fárias)—impress Texas Council with plans to invade Mexico to join Santa Anna resistance among northern Mexican liberals.

December 6   Mexía plan, approved by Council but vetoed on the ninth by Governor Smith: "I consider it bad policy to trust Mexicans ... we will in the end find them treacherous."

December 10   Council unanimously overruled Smith's veto.

December 5–10   Volunteers at San Antonio, led by Ben Milam who died in the fight, capture the town and the Alamo, and Cós retires below the Rio Grande promising never to return.

December 10   Council orders Mexía to San Antonio; he refuses, insisting on an invasion of prosperous Mexican port of Matamoros.

December 17   Sam Houston issues order to Bowie to organize Matamoros venture.

December 25   Council urges Smith to expedite Houston in organizing Matamoros campaign. Cós encounters at Laredo advance guard of new army Santa Anna is sending into Texas.

1836

January 6	In confusion over Matamoros venture—and in view of hesitation of Houston and Governor Smith—the Council orders Volunteer army, mostly at Alamo, under Francis Johnson to proceed on the Matamoros campaign.
January 7	Johnson reneges, swayed by Smith; Council appoints Fannin to take charge.
January 8	Johnson switches again; Council reappoints him, without relieving Fannin of command.
January 9–11	Governor Smith (acting on a letter of protest from Colonel Neill) berates Council. Council deposes him; Smith appeals for reconciliation; refused, he keeps government seals and dissolves Council, which nonetheless continues to act.
January 17	Houston orders Bowie to Alamo to blow it up and remove guns to Goliad and Gonzales.
January 21	Houston stalls Matamoros venture but takes furlough to make treaty with the Cherokees.
January 22	General Urrea occupies Matamoros with enough men to check any Texas attack there.
February 2	Bowie and Neill decide against abandoning Alamo.
February 2	William B. Travis arrives at Alamo; sides with Bowie and Neill to retain it as key defense.
February 8	Davy Crockett arrives at the Alamo with his twelve Tennessee Mounted Volunteers.
February 12	Santa Anna reaches Rio Grande, rests there four days. Fannin retires to Goliad. Travis and Bowie battle for command at Alamo.
February 16	Santa Anna sets out from Laredo for San Antonio de Béxar.
February 21	Santa Anna arrives at the Medina, 8 miles from San Antonio, at 2 P.M. Most of the army in camp by 5 P.M., but immobilized by heavy rain.
February 22	Santa Anna rests his troops; Washington's Birthday.
February 23	Siege of the Alamo begins.